From The Ghetto
To The Throne

Escaping My Own Prison

*This book is dedicated to
my mother, Rosa Thomas-Washington.
Words can't express the love I have for you.*

From The Ghetto
To The Throne
Escaping My Own Prison

Written By
Secret Bryant

Cover Photos By
Tanjanika Cook
and **Nicole Porter**

Cover Designs By
Salem Victoria *and*
Sun Child Wind Spirit

Edited By
Mylia Tiye Mal Jaza

FROM THE GHETTO TO THE THRONE:
Escaping My Own Prison

Copyright © 2016, Secret Bryant
All Rights Reserved.

ISBN-10: 1532949103   ISBN-13: 978-1532949104

Author Contact
Mr. Sammy Bryant
(360) 980-6153
secretbooks01@gmail.com
www.sostylesandbarber.com

Imprint of Record
CreateSpace On-Demand Publishing
7290-B Investment Drive
Charleston, SC 29418
4900 LaCross Road
North Charleston, SC 29406

Self-Publishing Associate
BePublished.Org - Chicago
Dr. Mary M. Jefferson
(972) 880-8316
www.bepublished.org
mari@bepublished.org

First Edition. Series Volume One.
Printed In the USA.
Recycled Paper Encouraged.

- TABLE OF CONTENT -

Acknowledgements

I would first like to thank God Almighty for loving and forgiving me more than I could ever deserve. I want to thank Him for allowing the Holy Spirit to guide me through life and also this book.

To my husband: I want to say thank you for allowing me to drag you down every adventurous journey that has ever popped up in my head. Thank you for how you have been my #1 Fan no matter what. Most of all, I thank you for trusting the God in me and allowing me the freedom to serve Him. This definitely makes life easier (lol).

To my mother: You have been right there since the day I was born, loving and caring for me. Thank you so much!

To my family (the Thomas, Bryant and Finley families), thank you. To Joyce Finley and Lillie Bryant: You two women were responsible for raising my loving husband. Thank you. R.I.H.

I also extend gratitude to all my babies. To Nette, my chocolate drop: I love you more than words can express. You have always been that force that drives me to get up and do something. Thank you for blessing me with my "Chris's" and One.

To my brother: I thank you for stepping up to the plate and being that father figure I need as a young girl trying to find her way back home. I love you.

I am grateful for my cousin Kathy, who has supported me even when she shouldn't have (*you know what I'm talking about*); my sisters, Patsy and Ola; my Southern Styles & Barber Family; all my nieces, nephews, cousins, and my friends. If I forgot any one, charge it to my head and not my heart.

I especially acknowledge the continuous blessing to my life represented by my late Aunt Joy, who inspired the title for this book. I love you. R.I.H.

Chapter One

"Let her come over here NOW," Rika screamed.

The doctor released her mother's arm so she could walk over to the side of her bed.

After the nurse finished checking Rika's cervix, she took off her gloves and washed her hands. She said, "She's ready for delivery!"

When they wheeled Rika into the delivery room, she was blinded by all the bright lights that were in that big room. Rika tried to open her eyes to see where she was, but she couldn't. All she could hear was her mother and the doctor making small talk about her giving birth. She didn't care about none of that.

"I just want them to get this baby out of me!"

On January 1, 1987 (at 11:20 a.m.), Rika gave birth to a four-pound, 10-ounce baby girl whom she named Nila LaShya. Even though it was a new year, it was the end of what was left of Rika's sanity. Over the next few months, she experienced a great deal of emotional stress. She found out later it was called "Post-Partum Depression." Rika was only thirteen, so she didn't understand what all that meant. And, for the record, neither did her mother because she didn't even think there was a problem. Rika remembered going in the bathroom and crying. What she would think to herself was, *I was having a bad day.* Or, *You're a baby with a baby.*

Some family members would wait until Rika's mother would leave and then talk about her. They knew, if they did this around her mother, she would go ballistic. She acted like a pit bull when it came her kids, period. The only thing that kept Rika from going crazy was the older boys thought she was sexy (at least, that's what she thought). Rika didn't really have many female friends. Since she had a baby at a young age, she was considered a hoe. That really didn't bother her none, because Rika was too familiar with that word.

It all started when Rika had just turned twelve years old. Her mother had moved them all the way to Texarkana, Texas. It was there that Rika met Trisha Wilson, and they hit it off instantly. Now, all the boys loved her. She had the prettiest coffee cream skin and dark brown eyes. She stood about 5'5" with a small waist, and her hair was short and sassy.

"See if your mother will let you go walking on Saturday," Trisha said while digging in her purse, searching for some lip gloss.

Rika already knew what that meant because it seemed like they went on these little missions every weekend. Trisha had sex with a different boy all the time. She said this was how she relieved her stress.

"Okay, but this time don't take as long as you did last time," Rika said, very irritated.

"You can't rush good sex."

"How come you can't? You did with Anthony Hopkins!"

"That was different. He had a little dick, so I just simply told his ass to get off me."

"Well, I'm not going to be sitting there looking like a runaway slave."

This time, Rika gave her a more serious look.

"You won't, don't worry. This time, I have a surprise for you!"

"I know you don't think I'm having sex. Now, that's what I'm not going to do. Shit my mother would kill me!"

Just the thought of that sent chills through Rika. They discussed all the necessary details, and headed towards the bus. It was a sunny spring afternoon, and the trees were already full. They met in front of the old Dollar Store where they always did, and headed to her next victim's house. On their way, Rika noticed a car following them. Trisha was too busy talking to even notice. She was taught at a young age to always watch her surroundings.

"Trisha, can you shut the hell up for a minute. There's a car that has been following us for the last few blocks," Rika said in a whisper, as if they could hear her.

"Where?" She asked, looking around nervously.

"Right over there, it's been following us a few blocks now."

Just then, a baby blue Cadillac pulled up on them. It was her mother's boyfriend.

"Don't say nothing, let me do the talking," she said, as if she were schooling Rika.

"Where you headed to Trisha?" Her mom's boyfriend asked with a smirk on his face.

"To the Boys & Girls Club."

"Do your momma know?" He asked, now laughing, as if he knew she was lying.

"I told her last night, and she said just be in before dark."

"Alright. Do you need a ride? Because, you're going the wrong way." With that, he let out a gut-busting laugh and drove off.

When they arrived at Jock's house, he was standing in the window as if he was waiting for their arrival. They walked up the stairs to his apartment that he shared with his cousin. Trisha and Rika went in and sat down on the couch, and looked around at the tiny space. On the walls were all sorts of posters of various celebrities -- Janet Jackson, Run DMC, The Fat Boys, and Slick Rick just to name a few. On the floor in the corner were the latest copies of *Playboy* and *Hustler* magazines, *Yuk!* Rika thought to herself, *All boys think about is sex. I don't really understand what all the hype is. All I know is people do whatever to get it.*

"Damn girl, you look fly as hell in those jeans, can we get this party started?" Jock blurted, glaring at her with lustful eyes.

"Not so fast, silly. We have to wait for Boogie to come back so he can keep my girl company," Trisha said, smiling as if she was doing Rika a favor.

"I guess so. If you ask me, she looks like a big girl that can handle herself."

Before he could speak another word, the door swung open and a fine ass brotha entered the room. *Damn, he fine as hell! I might just consider this one*, Rika thought to herself. Boogie walked in with a bottle of Old English 800 in one hand a joint in the other. He was as smooth as chocolate, with deep dimples that jumped right out at Rika. His hair was in a bald fade with lines going across the side of his head. His teeth were dripping gold on the top four teeth.

"What we got going on in here?" Boogie asked, with his eyes glued on Jock.

"Man, I need you to do me a favor, and keep baby girl company for me while I take care of this piece right quick," Jock said.

He smiled, and he too had dimples. So, Rika could see clearly that they were related.

"Oh, yeah! Why do I have to babysit all the time? I want to party to," Boogie said, looking at her as if he was waiting for her to respond.

"Are you gone do it or not, man?"

At this point, Jock was getting agitated.

"Yeah, man."

"Thanks."

With that, he disappeared in the room.

"Well, what's your name?" Boogie asked.

"Rika," she said, with emphasis on the 'R'.

"Rika," he repeated. "Well how old are you?"

Without hesitation, she said, "Fifteen."

He shot her a puzzled look as he sat down on the couch next to her. Rika could smell his cologne mixed with malt liquor, but his presence still sent waves through her body. Now, that was the first time she had ever had a physical attraction to anyone of the opposite sex, and it felt good.

"You don't look fifteen, maybe twelve or thirteen. Anyway, are you comfortable?" He asked, staring her straight in the face like he was looking right through her.

"No, I'm fine," Rika said, staring right back at him.

"Do you smoke?" He asked, handing her the joint.

She shot him a look that could kill, raised her eyebrow, and shook her head no.

"Don't bite my head off. I just asked a question. Do you have a boy friend?" He asked a little calmer.

"No, and I'm not interested in one either. I am trying to focus on school right now, and the only thing that would do is complicate things."

Rika was trying to sound as intelligent as she possibly could. That was one of the reasons why Trisha took Rika with her. She said that Rika didn't act childish like the rest of their friends. The truth was, Rika didn't have a boyfriend that she could screw around with like the rest of their friends whose men Trisha had slept with.

"Oh shit, sound like you a good girl. Well, that's good. Don't get caught up in all this shit here either," Boogie said, holding up his refreshments.

Over the next hour, they sat around laughing and making small talk about different topics. Just when Rika thought things were going smooth, he asked, "Have you ever had sex before?"

Before she could say a word, Trisha opened the door. *Yes, saved by the bell*, Rika thought. When her eyes met Trisha's, there was a strange look in them that Rika just couldn't quit figure out. She jumped up and ran over to Trisha. With fear written all over her face, she finally spoke.

"What the hell happened? Are you okay? Why are you looking like you just got hit by an 18-wheeler?" Rika asked, sounding like she was interrogating Trisha.

"No, I'm fine. How 'bout you, are you okay?" Trisha asked, like she was in shock.

Jock came out of the room with a washcloth in his hand and a look that would kill on his face.

"Let's ride, man. I gotta go check on something across town," he said, then motioned for Boogie.

Now Boogie had the same look on his face as Rika did. He looked at her and asked, "You straight? You need a ride or something?"

Rika was confused as hell at this point. That was not the response that she was used to seeing. Normally, boys begged to be in Trisha's presence, but this vibe was different. Before Rika could speak a word, Jock interrupted.

"Hell naw, man. I got shit to do. And naw, they walked over here, they can walk back."

With that, he opened the door, letting them know it was time to move around. On they way home, Trisha and Rika walked in silence. Rika was in deep thought about this little tingle that she felt when she was in the company of Boogie. Rika wanted to ask Trisha about it, but the thought quickly faded away.

When they finally made it to Trisha's house, her little sister and her friends were sitting on the porch. Geisha was an 11-year-old know-it-all and the leader of the pack. What she said went when it came to her friends.

"Where you been, Trisha?"

"None of your business. Is momma here?" She said with attitude.

"No, she's at the shop. What's wrong with you? You look like you have been getting dug in, and you smell like it to. Rika, why do you hang with her? You know she's a hoe!"

Geisha and her friends all laughed in unison.

"I ain't a hoe, and you better watch your mouth!" Trisha scolded.

"Don't be mad. I want to be a hoe too when I get big," Geisha said, like there was a class available.

One of her friends spoke up, "Me too! They make a lot of money! My auntie is one, and she got men beating down her door begging her to take their money."

"That's what's up," Geisha shot back, like it was the thing to do.

"Well, I'm not. I'm going to be a nurse like momma. Now, she makes a LOT of money," the girl sitting on her bike said.

"Well, I'm glad to see at least one of your friends have some sense. Besides, you not gonna be a hoe either, so stop being stupid. Did anybody call for me?" Trisha said while looking down at the mail she had in her hand.

"Yeah, some girl called and said to tell you to stop fucking her man! Syke! Just some boy who wouldn't give me his name, so I hung up on him, and Leon."

Now, Leon was her mother's boyfriend. And, Rika just didn't understand why he would be calling for Trisha when they had just seen him hours before. Rika dismissed the thought, *Because, maybe her mom had him check in on her.*

On that note, Trisha and Rika walked in the house, and Rika headed straight to the kitchen to get her something to drink. Trisha's mom had a nice place. The entire house was plush, with red and black leather furniture and matching pictures. In the corner were a floor model television and a picture of Trisha's family with colored flowers surrounding it. Trisha's mom was a hair stylist at the local salon where she spent most of her time. What was left of it, she was over at her boyfriend's house. Trisha had the responsibility of taking care of her two sisters, which she often complained about.

"I don't know why I always have to keep them, with they bad asses. Geisha don't listen to shit I say, and all Brittany want to do is eat and watch cartoons," she complained.

"Why don't you say something? I would." Rika told her.

"It's no use, all she says is that she's working to take care of us. And, believe me, I do understand. But why don't she come get us on her days off is what I don't understand. Instead, she spends her free time over to Leon's house, leaving me to take care of her responsibilities. I promise you, you are lucky to have your mom there when you come home, and when you wake up.

"It's hard when you never get to spend time with your mom," Trisha continued. "We never talk about how school was or how was my day. It's just, 'Make sure they get their bath. Make sure they eat.' But if something happens, I'm the one she blames because I'm the oldest."

As they entered Trisha's room, Rika stood by the door while Trisha cleared a spot for Rika to sit on the foot of her bed.

"Are you going to tell me what happened with you and Jock?" Rika tried to choose the right words.

"He's a jerk," she spat.

"Well, what the hell happened? I mean it can't be that bad."

She looked at Rika like she was her worst enemy.

"Never mind, you don't have to," Rika said, still standing.

"I'm sorry, it's not your fault. It's just I've never been treated like that before," Trisha said.

"Are you going to tell me, or do I have to beat it out of you?" Rika asked, now annoyed.

"He asked me to suck his dick, and when I said, 'No,' he got mad and rammed his dick in me so hard it felt like he was ripping my pussy to shreds. The more I begged him to stop, the harder he got until my whole body became numb."

"Well, why didn't you scream or something?" Rika asked with a look of fear on her face.

She got so close to Rika that Rika could smell the chips Trisha ate earlier on her breath. With a devilish grin on her face, she said, "I kinda liked it. The part that I didn't like was when he was choking me and saying things like, 'Next time I tell you to do something, do it,' and 'Whose pussy is this?' And, when I didn't answer, he got harder. For a minute, I didn't answer just so he could go harder."

She let out a childish giggle. Rika just rolled her eyes and changed the subject. The truth of the matter was, he didn't have a problem she did. Rika stood there for a moment in her own thoughts, imagining herself wrapped up in Boogie's arms. She could still smell his cologne up her nostrils. Her thought was interrupted when the door closed and Trisha was standing directly in front of her.

"Earth calling Rika. What the hell are you thinking about?" She said with her hands on her hips.

"Nothing. Just thinking about what I'm wearing to church tomorrow. My momma want me in early today so I can be ready," Rika lied.

"If I tell you something, you promise not to tell?" Trisha asked with sincerity written all over her face.

"What? You tell me everything anyway, so why do I have to promise?" Rika responded.

"Just promise." She repeated.

"I promise," Rika said, really wanting to know.

"I had sex with Leon," she said and looked at Rika, waiting for a response.

But the shock wouldn't let her speak or move. She continued without hesitation.

"One day I had just got out of the shower and he walked in. He stood there for a minute like he was shocked. I grabbed the towel, trying to cover myself, but it was too late. I saw his eyes when they left mine and stopped on my breasts, and then he quickly looked away.

"Days later, I heard him and my mother in the room having sex – and, from the sounds of things, they were both excited with pleasure. I couldn't fall asleep because they were so loud, like no one was in the house but them. I tossed and turned for a minute and, for some reason, I got real moist between my legs then I drifted off to sleep. That night I dreamed that me and Leon had sex. When I woke up, my nipples were hard and I was wet as hell. The dream seemed so real.

"The next morning, my mother was running late for work and she instructed me to get my sisters on the bus. When I got them off to school, I started getting ready for school. I had just pulled up my panties when the door opened. It was Leon. This time, he stood there and asked if I needed a ride to school? My body did things that I couldn't control, because the next thing I know, I was walking over to him caressing my own body, asking him if he liked what he saw. He slowly nodded his head yes, and dropped his head then walked out," Trisha said.

"On the ride to school, he acted like nothing happened. I asked him was he going to tell my momma and he assured me that he wouldn't. After school, I was laying on the couch watching 'Good Times' when I heard a key being put in the lock. It turned and then it opened. It was him again, only this time he had been drinking.

"He asked if there was any mail for my mother. As I got up to get it, I dropped the remote. When I bent down to pick it up, I felt his hand between my legs, and it felt great! I turned around and gave him a wet sloppy kiss, as we began to breathe long and deep. He touched me so gentle but firm, and I could feel his pants rise," Trisha confessed.

"I started unbuttoning his pants while he took off his shirt. My body was screaming for more of his attention and I could hardly wait for him to be inside of me. He carried me over to the couch, and it was my turn to be undressed. He had to peel my pants off because they were soaking wet. I could feel his tongue slide up and down my body until it stopped at the beginning of my hairline. That was the first time I ever experienced oral sex.

"Before I knew it, my whole body shook with excitement. I tried to cover me face from embarrassment, but I quickly took my hands away when I felt him going inside of me. I couldn't help moaning! The shit was good, so I opened my legs as wide as they could go so I could receive all of him. He was bigger than anyone I had ever been with, but I didn't care. He took his hand and started playing with my clit until I exploded, and he followed right behind me.

"He got up and got dressed. And before he left, he turned around and said, 'It's our little secret. Now, go take a long hot bath and don't give my pussy to nobody else. You hear me?' And I did just what I was told. Every since then, he's been giving me money and buying me all kinds of gifts," she finished, with her face in her hands.

Rika was stunned! Her mouth couldn't open. In fact, Rika thought she was going to pass out from lack of oxygen to her brain. With her mouth suddenly wide open, she slid to the floor to keep from falling. Finally able to breathe, she mumbled.

"Can I have a drink of water?" Rika asked, never looking at Trisha.

Trisha got up, went to the kitchen, and then returned.

"You won't judge me will you? I mean, honestly, I don't feel bad except for the fact that he's momma's boyfriend," she said.

Rika stood up, feeling weak in the knees and simply said, "Only God can judge you," and walked out.

Over the next few months, Rika's relationship with Trisha slowly faded away. She still called from time to time, telling her about the different events that were happening in her life. Rika kept her word, she didn't tell anybody and, most important, she didn't judge her. The real reason for their separation was there were a lot of things going on with her as well. She'd lost her first cousin, and Rika had recently changed schools.

Rika had been at Pine Street Middle School for a couple of months before she even considered meeting anyone. The girls there seemed to be a little out of her league, that was until the day she met Yolanda. They had a lot in common. She was the same age as Rika. She was the baby of her family but, most of all, she was a virgin just like Rika. They used to imagine things like what it would be like to have sex with a boy. But, just like Rika, she was scared.

Her mother was a nurse and worked late hours, so Yolanda spent a lot of time over at her sister's house. Now, Yolanda was a short plump sista with big hips. Her weight was in all the right places though, and she had pretty brown skin and light brown eyes with shoulder-length curly hair.

Rika really couldn't understand why she wore make-up because she was naturally beautiful. But when she put it on, the shit was flawless.

"Are you going to the fair this weekend?" She asked while they were in the lunch line getting their favorite (nachos).

"Probably so. My momma said I could, but I need to get me something to wear. How 'bout you? Are you going?" She said, paying for her food.

Right then, Chanel walked up slowly trying to scare them. Chanel was very sassy. She had long hair that she never combed, creamy-colored skin, and thin lips. Chanel didn't really know her own beauty, she was different from the two of them. She didn't care about her appearance at all. She wore wrinkled clothes to school, and sometimes they wondered if Chanel even brushed her teeth before she left the house. Rika couldn't understand why Chanel carried herself like that because she was beautiful inside and out.

"What y'all getting? Oh, I see, the famous nachos. Well, I'll go over and save us some seats. Get my lunch and I'll meet y'all over there," Chanel said as she disappeared through the crowd.

That was another thing about her. She never had lunch money, and they didn't mind because all she had to do was say the word and they would buy her lunch.

"What's up for this weekend?" Chanel asked as they sat down across from her.

"That's what we were trying to figure out," Yolanda said, biting down on one of her chips.

"Chanel, you think your mom will let you go?" Rika said, now digging in herself.

"Yeah, but I would have to spend the night at one of you guy's house because my mother works on Saturday."

"How about both of you stay at my house," Yolanda suggested. "My mother won't be there, and I won't have to go to my sisters house."

"Cool. I'm with it. I'll ask my mom when I get home," Rika said, taking a drink of her strawberry soda.

"Let's have some boys over!" Chanel said with excitement.

Chanel was the one in the crew that talked like she knew so much about sex. She would tell them of the different boys she slept with, but Yolanda and Rika knew otherwise. She was a virgin just like them. She just wanted to feel important.

"What you think, Rika? I'm down to tease a little." Yolanda asked Rika.

See, they had mastered the art of being a good tease. But when it was time to go to second base, the answer was, "No!"

"I don't care. Who are we going to invite?" Rika replied.

"Let's invite Rodney and his crew," Chanel said, looking at the table right behind where they were sitting.

"Hell no!" Yolanda and Rika said at the same time.

"I know who," Yolanda said, wiping her hands on a napkin.

"Who?" Chanel and Rika asked.

"I'll tell you later, after I hook it up," Yolanda said.

They all stood up to go throw their trash away. They said their good byes and headed to class. Once Saturday came and they had left the fair, they were all sitting around on the floor watching the movie "Crush Groove." Chanel broke the silence.

"So, did you make that hook-up for us?" She asked as she stood up and pulled her pajamas up.

They both glared at Yolanda, waiting for her response.

"It's all taken care of," she stated.

"Well, who the fuck is it?" Rika said, getting very impatient.

"Damn, calm down. You'll see," Yolanda said.

Just then, they heard a slight tap on the door. They all looked at each other like they weren't expecting anyone. Yolanda went to answer the door, while Chanel and Rika ran to the bathroom to freshen up. While they were in the bathroom, Rika could feel her whole attitude change from "junior high school" to "straight sexy."

Rika pulled her hair into a ponytail, and rubbed her body down with her new perfume oil by Art Row Classic that her Aunt Hope sent her from California. The shit smelled delicious. They walked out of the bathroom and could hear the sound of dudes talking. One of the voices sounded familiar. When Rika entered the room, her heart dropped.

"What's up, Rika?" Boogie said with a smile as wide as the I-35 freeway.

Rika played it off, as if Boogie's presence didn't matter. She hadn't seen Boogie since the incident with Trisha at Jock's apartment some months ago.

"What's up?" Rika said very nonchalantly.

"You know him, Rika?" Chanel asked her, looking very curious.

"No, I don't know him like that. I met him one day a few months ago. We chopped it up for about an hour or so and that was it. End of story."

She sat down on one of Yolanda's mom's dinette chairs with her legs crossed, looking and feeling ever so sexy.

"Don't say it like that. You make it sound like you didn't enjoy yourself, like I was boring or something. Is that what you are saying?" Boogie asked, looking at her as if she had offended him.

"No, not like that. It's just that she's asking me like something happened between us, and I'm just stating the facts. I didn't mean to offend you," Rika said, now more humble.

"No problem. Now, what do I have to do to get you to come sit next to me so we can finish the conversation we were having that day? And, by the way, you looking good these days. Hold up a minute. Where's your other sidekick?" He asked, getting even more comfortable and taking off his jacket.

"We don't talk like that no more. So, I guess she's doing fine," she said as she stood up and made her way over to the couch where he was sitting.

"Well, now that we got that out of the way, John and Pete, this is Chanel and Rika. Ladies, these are the fellas," Yolanda said.

They all said hello, and everybody started getting acquainted. For the next hour, they all just sat and finished watching the rest of the movie. When it was over, Yolanda stood up and asked if they wanted something to drink. As she made her way to the kitchen, Rika quickly followed, leaving Chanel to entertain.

"How do you know them?" Rika whispered.

"I know Jason and Pete. I don't know the other guy, but it seems like you do. And, damn he's fine as hell," Yolanda said as she poured each of them a glass of juice.

When the cups were filled, they picked up the glasses and turned to exit. Then, they looked at each other and said at the same time, "It's show time!"

Chanel was talking a mile a minute. They could tell she was nervous because she kept licking her lips.

"Hey, Chanel, come to the bathroom real quick," Rika told her.

Before she stood up, Pete grabbed Chanel by the hand and said, "Don't take too long!"

Rika rolled her eyes and headed towards the bathroom. While in there, she put some lip gloss on and handed it to Chanel. She then sprayed on some body spray and passed that to her as well. She popped a piece of gum in her mouth and handed a piece to Chanel. This was the only way Rika could make sure Chanel was straight without embarrassing her because she was very sensitive. Before they made it back to the front room, she grabbed her by the arm, looking like she had seen a ghost.

"What if he wants to have sex?"

Rika laughed and said, "I know you're not worried about that. I should be asking you that. Remember, I'm a virgin not you!"

Rika laughed and walked into the living room. Jason and Yolanda didn't waste any time. They were already in Yolanda's room. Rika sat back down next to Boogie, and they started talking.

"So, how have you been, lil momma?" He inquired real low.

She could tell he had just hit some weed because his eyes were red and tight, plus the aroma instantly attacked her nostrils.

"I've been good. I'm trying to make the cheerleading team for next year. And, what have you been up too?"

"Not much, just trying to keep my head up. I just got a job, so I've been working a lot. In fact, this is my first weekend off since I started. That's why, when these clowns ask me to bring them over here, I almost said 'no' but I'm glad I came -- especially now that I see you," he said with a naughty grin.

Rika smiled back because she felt the same way. *It couldn't have worked out any better than this.* Just then, Pete took Chanel by the hand and started leading her to the other room as if that was his house. Boogie looked at Rika and they laughed.

"So, you never answered my question," he said, rubbing her face with the back of his hand.

"What question?" She asked like she didn't know.

"Are you a virgin?" With that, he lifted her chin up so he could look her in the eyes.

"Yes," she said softly.

Rika liked telling boys that. That way, if she didn't go through with it, she could use that as the excuse. Boogie let his head rest on the back of the couch before he spoke another word.

"I'm tired. Does she have a blanket I can use?"

She got up and got a blanket out of the hall closet. When Rika returned, he was stretched out on the couch with his eyes closed. She shook him and handed him the blanket, then she turned to walk away. *Damn! I knew I shouldn't have told him that.* She could have kicked herself.

Rika felt him grab her hand, and then he said, "Aren't you going to lay down and keep me company?"

She smiled and walked in his direction. He opened up the cover so she could slide in front of him. As they laid there holding each other, she could feel his breathing getting heavy and he fell asleep. She smiled to herself, because for some reason she felt safe. So, Rika snuggled in even closer and dosed off.

It seemed like she had just dosed off when she felt his hand under her shirt trying to slide her bra up to expose her melons. But, she laid there like she didn't feel a thing. He shook her softly to see if she would respond. She did.

"What's up?" Rika asked, trying to sound like he had woke her up.

"Listen, you think I can have a kiss?"

He sounded like he needed it. So, she wrapped her arms around his neck and laid it on him. It was soft and sweet. It sent electric waves through her entire body -- from head to toe.

"Your lips sure are soft. You sure you haven't had sex with anybody because, that damn sure didn't feel like I was kissing any virgin?" He said all while sucking her bottom lip.

"I didn't say that I never kissed before. I just said I haven't had sex before."

Rika was now sticking her tongue in his mouth, and grinding her hips at the same time. She knew that she was a good kisser because she practiced on her dolls when she was little. But, hearing it from a human, made it official.

"Stop, don't do that. I don't want you to do something you will regret later, but, at the same time, I'm still a man," he said, trying to back up some.

"You don't have to worry. Nothing's going to happen," Rika said with assurance.

"Oh, I get it. You like to tease niggas and get them all aroused, then tell them 'no,' then they gotta go home and soak in cool water to keep from getting blue balls."

They both laughed. Then, he got serious.

"You can't do me like that. No. I'm not going to take it because I don't have to. I know how to make you give it to me, and then I will be in control."

"How old are you anyway?"

He pulled her bra back down. The choice of words he used, and the tone in his voice, shook her for a minute.

"You sure you want to know?"

Rika nodded her head up and down. He climbed on top of her and said, "Eighteen," then he gave her a long deep kiss and began to grind her in the right spot. She could feel him getting excited, and this made her want him even more. He took her by her hand and put it on his rod, and motioned for her to stroke it. She did. Before he let her up, she thought she would explode. And Boogie was right. Rika did want to beg him not to stop, but he did anyway.

"See, I told you I can make you give it to me. I didn't want to do you like that, but I had to. From now on, remember this: Don't pre-heat the oven if you not going to put nothing in it," Boogie said.

With that, he got up and went to the bathroom. And, left her laying on the couch in total shock.

Chapter Two

It was raining cats and dogs in Wichita, Kansas, and Showboat was in the garage admiring his new red Suzuki moped his parents had bought him for Easter. He was so excited because he was the only kid in town to have one. Showboat was his father's first-born son, and his mother's only child, so he was spoiled rotten. His mom promised him this gift only if he would not get kicked out of school, like he had so many times in the past.

It was her way of encouraging him to do better. Since his mom had him at such an early age, he lived with his grandmother, who treated him like her very own. His mother was a professional hustler and was good at it, which landed her in jail most of his young life. When she was out doing her thing, she would bring him all kinds of expensive gifts. She thought that would make up for her absence, but she was wrong. As a young boy, all Showboat wanted was his mother, and nothing could compare to the time they spent together when she was out on the street.

Now, his father on the other hand, was a hard worker who had good job working for Beech Aircraft and he was pimping on the side. Showboat loved his daddy dearly, so when his mom wasn't around, all he wanted was his dad. He looked up to his dad because he liked the way he handled the ladies. That was his hero and he wanted to be just like him when he grew up.

Showboat was very intelligent even at a young age. You couldn't do anything around him because he was a fast learner. Destined for success, he picked up his suave and charming demeanor from his dad and older uncles who were also in the pimp game. Too young to start his own pimp ring, he directed his attention to something more on his level. He directed his attention to fighting. He didn't really go around picking fights, but he damn sure finished them.

One day, he was at Spruce Park playing basketball with some of the local boys. The game got a little heated, one thing lead to another, and before it was over with, he had to fight all three boys. Feeling good about his victory, he went home like nothing ever happened. Even though he loved to fight, there was something else he loved even more, the ladies.

Showboat had a serious crush on a girl at his school named Kameisha who had just moved to the town from New York. Kameisha was light skinned with pretty hair that she kept pulled in a ponytail, her eyes were so slanted he thought she was a Black China doll. Her mother was very protective of her, so the only way he could get close to her was through her brother, Warnis aka Fiz. He would make up excuses to go see her. But, when he got to her door, he would ask for his new sidekick and their mom would welcome him in. Kameisha's mother quickly caught on to his mischief though.

"Why is this little boy hanging around my house? I know he ain't over here for my daughter," she said entering the house with her sister close behind her.

"No ma'am. I'm here for Fiz," he lied.

"Don't let me find out otherwise or you'll regret it, boy. You hear me?"

"Yes ma'am," Showboat said, now standing up, heading to Fiz's room.

It was a funny thing because Warnis and Kameisha shared rooms, which made things even that more convenient for Showboat to map out his plan. Kameisha's mother worked the 2-10 shift as a custodian for the Board of Education. That was during the time Showboat would make his move.

Once, Kameisha's mother worked the day shift. Kameisha was getting ready to go back to bed when the phone rang. It was Showboat.

"Hello," she answered in a sweet voice.

"What are you doing?" He asked in a maturing, deep voice.

"I'm tired, so I'm not going to school today," she said.

"Well, me either. I'll be over there in about five minutes."

He hung up the phone, making a mad dash to her house. Upon his arrival, she was there waiting because she knew what he wanted, and she wanted the same thing in return. He knocked, she opened the door, and they headed to her mother's room where she was watching TV. He crawled in the bed next to her, and pretended to be watching television with her. He knew his time was limited so he started French kissing her, then made his way to her neck and whispered in her ear letting her know that he wanted "to fuck" her. She turned to look at him, letting him know that he offended her by his choice of words.

"Why do you have to say that word? I don't like it."

"I'm sorry baby. I want to make love to you, because I really do love you," he said, all the while massaging her pussy.

Then he slid one finger inside her. He could tell she was getting into it by the way her legs loosened up. She was a virgin, so he wanted to take his time and be gentle so she would let him do it again. It was short, sweet and to the point. When they were finished, it was official, she was his girl and he was her man.

Over the next few months, things had changed a lot. They had gotten real close, and Kameisha didn't have a care in the world. She knew she had won his heart. No other girl in the school had what she had. She was 4'7" with a flat stomach, curvy hips, and a size D bra cup that Showboat appreciated. She knew it because she always found his hands under her shirt, twirling her nipples between his two fingers.

"Damn, girl. You got some big titties, and they are so soft," he said, reminiscing on the night he first tasted them.

"I know," she said, trying to sound flirtatious.

What she didn't know was that Showboat was not only fine as hell to her, there were a few other girls that felt the same way. On several occasions, he would creep off and hit them too. He was accustomed to being with different chicks at the same time because this was what he grew up watching from the men in his family. No doubt in his mind that he loved her, but there was just something about having multiple women around him. It eased some of the pain he'd experienced in his life up to that point.

A few years earlier, Showboat was in the yard playing with his two uncles. Randy was a couple of years older than him, and Shawty was one year younger than him. They would always see who could jump out of their room window the fastest. Their room was located on the second floor of his grandmother's four-bedroom house. The house was occupied by Showboat's four uncles, two aunts, and his grandparents. Since Randy, Showboat and Shawty didn't have much of a front yard, they came up with this game. But, they all had their own motives too. They wanted to see who was the toughest.

It was a few days before Christmas, and the boys were all excited because of all the gifts under the tree. Showboat knew he had the most gifts because he saw when his dad dropped them off. His mother was in jail as usual, but that didn't seem to have an effect on him at this point. He just couldn't wait to tear into those gifts on Christmas day.

His grandmother was in the kitchen preparing desserts to accompany their dinner, and his grandfather had just come in from work. Showboat always sensed the tension between he and his grandfather. He always wanted to prove that his boys were tougher than Showboat was, and would sometime make them fight. A lot of the reason was because his grandfather was the breadwinner for the family and didn't appreciate the fact that he had to work his hands to the bone just to provide for his kids and take care of Showboat too.

It didn't make things better when Showboat's "Pops" would pull up in his brand new canary yellow drop-top convertible Oldsmobile 98. Flint, which was his street name, would step through the door cleaner than the Board of Health -- with his hair processed to a tee, and his Godfather cocked to the side. Flint never came empty handed, and that would burn Mr. Wilson up even though that was his own envy it still didn't have anything to do with Showboat.

That night, Mrs. Wilson did the usual and got her younger son and grandson ready for bed. This particular night, they had some other relatives over. They all ended up spending the night over there because they were having lots of fun, so Mrs. Wilson tucked them in as well. While in their room, they did what most children did -- laughed and played until they had to get their asses beat to help them fall to sleep faster.

Someone must have forgotten to turn the Christmas lights off on the tree. Because, sometime during the night, the tree caught fire. The smell of smoke awoke Showboat, so he got up and woke everybody up and told them he smelled smoke. His Uncle Bobbo got up and tried to go downstairs with his little brothers, nephews and cousins right behind him. They couldn't go far. The smoke was so hot, they had to go back upstairs. That's when Randy, Shawty and Showboat's little game came in handy because they were forced to jump out of the window.

By the time they all made it safely out of the window, his grandparents were already standing in the front yard. Mrs. Wilson and her oldest son, Bobbo, both re-entered the house to get the smaller children left inside safely out to the yard. Once inside the house, the smaller children were located and quickly brought outside where Mrs. Wilson and Bobbo began giving them CPR. Mr. Wilson was standing out front trying to put the fire out with the water hose that he had in his front yard.

By the time the fire department arrived, the fire was burning out of control and Mrs. Wilson had suffered from first-degree burns from when she went back into the house to save her grandbabies. The firefighters just stood there not doing a thing. They claimed the water hydrant was frozen due to the cold weather. Showboat sat inside the broken down Pontiac with the rest of the kids and watched in disbelief. He watched as his grandmother knocked on the neighbor's door for help, with her skin falling off and exposing the pink of her flesh.

Before the morning had come, two babies were dead, two children were burned severely, and Mrs. Wilson was also terribly burned. During the months to follow, the family suffered a great deal of grief. Four months later, Mrs. Wilson was finally put to rest due to complications she suffered from her burns. Showboat loved his grandmother more than life itself. Now, where would he go? Who would take care of him? His mother couldn't because she was still in and out of jail. The only person that he could think of was his Pops, but instead he was forced to go to Kansas City to live with his auntie.

Living with Aunt Felicia wasn't a picnic either. Showboat had to clean, wash clothes, and tend to his little cousin also burned in the fire. Over the next two years, Showboat couldn't think of anything more than to see the day they finally considered letting him go to stay with his father. He didn't understand what all the fuss was about, with him not being able to stay there.

There were times, when he was younger, that his Pops would come get him so they could spend time together. Showboat seemed to love these outings. When it was time for him to go home, he always wanted to go spend the night at his dad's house. His dad would often say things like, "You gotta go home." Or, even worse, he would send him inside the corner store to get candy and, once inside the store, his dad would pull off. When Showboat came out of the store and saw that his Pops had left him, he would drop his head and cry all the way back home.

The truth was, Mrs. Wilson wasn't having it when she was alive. *What was the problem now*? He wondered. This made Showboat rebel even more. He thought that it would help him get the attention he wanted from his parents faster. But, the only thing it got him was a well-kicked ass.

One day, Showboat came in from school and sat down to do his homework when the phone rang. It was Pat, his mom.

"Hello," he answered.

"Hey baby! What you doing?" She said in a sad voice.

He answered, "Doing my homework. When are you coming to get me? I don't like it here."

In a shocking tone, she asked, "Why? What's going on?"

Showboat said, "Because she's always beating on me! I get in trouble for stuff Nikki tells her, and I'm just tired of her shit. And why can't I just go with my Pops anyway?"

"What the hell did you just say? Felicia knows I don't play that shit, putting her hands on my fucking son and shit! I'll kill her fucking ass," Pat exclaimed.

Now, Showboat knew that there was some truth to that, because his mom was crazy as hell. And, Felicia knew it too. They were sisters, and they had fistfights all the time when they were younger. Now, what Pat couldn't understand was why her "niece was snitching on her cousin when they were so close." When Showboat and Nikki were younger, they would tell people that they were brother and sister. Pat knew she had to get her son out of there. He had already been through enough.

"I tell you what. Why don't you come to Topeka and stay down here with me? I've been doing pretty well -- I have a job, and I have my own place now. So, what do you think?" Pat asked.

Showboat could hardly believe his ears. Finally he was getting out of what he considered a hellhole. Without hesitation he accepted his mother's invitation. That night, as he laid in bed, he kept wondering what it would be like staying with mom because that was something he'd never done before. After giving it a little more thought, he became angry. *If she had a job and her own place, why haven't she been came and got me?* He wondered. Then, he let the thought vanish because he really didn't care what her reason was. *She is coming now.*

Chapter Three

Rika was on her way to visit her friend she hadn't seen in a while, when she ran into one of her classmates, Laconia. Laconia was a foster child who sometimes went through several different foster homes in a year. She wasn't somebody Rika would normally stop and chat with but, this time, she made an exception.

"Where are you headed, Rika?" she asked, running up behind her out of breath.

"Just walking. Where are you coming from?" Rika said, trying to sound like she was interested.

"Over Jock's house, and going back to smoke some weed. You want to come?"

Rika's eyes lit up. *Hell yeah!* She wanted to go. Trying to sound unsure, she said, "I don't know. I don't smoke weed and I don't want to just be sitting around in y'all face. So, I guess I'll pass."

Laconia bit the bait, because she said just what Rika wanted to hear.

"You won't be sitting there by yourself. Jock has a fine ass cousin who lives there, so he can keep you company."

Trying not to answer too fast, "You sure it won't be a problem?"

"I'm sure."

They headed in the direction of some residential houses. Now, Rika didn't want to blow her cover, but that sure as hell wasn't the way Trisha and Rika went to get to the guys' apartment. Before Rika could give it any more thought, they stepped on the porch of a big brick house. Laconia knocked on the door. After a couple of knocks, Jock opened it.

"What's up, Laconia. Who's your friend?" Jock said while opening the door so they could come in.

Jock kept staring at Rika. He felt like he knew her from somewhere, but he couldn't put his finger on it.

"Rika, this is Jock, and, Jock, this is Rika," Laconia said.

Rika extended her arm for a ladylike handshake.

"Cut the bullshit," Jock laughed.

"What bullshit?" Rika said trying to hold back her laughter.

Before she could say another word, Boogie came out of the kitchen. You would have thought he'd seen a ghost.

"Well, well, well. What's up, Rika? You know three times is a charm. So, what brings us to this crossroad again?"

"Okay. Is somebody going to tell me what the hell is going on?" Laconia looked at Rika with a demanding expression.

"I met Boogie and Jock a few months ago," she said.

"Oh, I thought they had the wrong person. Oh, well. What's up with the smoke, Jock?" Laconia said as she made her way to the couch.

"It's right here. You got something on it?" Jock held up the joint.

"Yeah, my lips, you jerk!"

She snatched the joint from his hand and he looked like he lost his best friend as he watched her put the fire to the end of it. All Rika could do was laugh, and watch Boogie out the corner of her eye while he went into the refrigerator and grabbed a beer.

"Rika, you still don't smoke?" Boogie asked.

"Nope," she replied, shaking her head at the same time.

Rika wanted to say more, but she was mesmerized at the sight of their house. It was nothing like the ratty apartment they had at first. The living room was huge, with flowers and plants hanging from the ceiling. In the corner against the wall, there was a statue of a giraffe, and on the opposite side of the wall was a tall statue of a lion. Their sofa was so soft and was the color of a crisp hundred-dollar bill. She kept finding herself running her fingers across the arm of it. On the floor, there was a gigantic throw rug with a picture of a jaguar on it.

Rika took it that was the theme. Rather, she thought they wanted you to feel like you were in a jungle. The fish tank was breathtaking. They had the most beautiful fish she had ever seen. Rika was so caught in the moment that she didn't hear what Laconia was saying. All she saw was her lips moving.

"What is on your mind? I've been asking you for the last five minutes, 'Do you want something to drink?'"

She blew smoke right in Rika's direction.

"My bad. But, no thank you."

"What's up, Rika? You don't want to talk to me or something?" Boogie said, rubbing her hair with his hands.

"Cool. What do you want to talk about? I mean, the last time I saw you, I didn't think you ever wanted to speak to me again."

For some reason, she could feel the tone in his voice change. "Never that. If nothing else, we always going to be friends. Deal?"

"That's right! Can I ask you something?"

"Anything," he said, scooting to the edge of his seat as if Rika had a secret that she was going to reveal.

"Can I have some Kool-Aid?"

Rika licked her lips like she was dying of thirst.

"There you go with that shit again. I done told you. But, guess what? Today might be your lucky day," he said.

"And just what does that suppose to mean?"

"Damn, can we get in on this conversation? Hell, y'all acting like we don't even exist," Jock said, rolling another joint.

"Hell yeah. What? Are we invisible or what? Damn, if I didn't know any better, I'd think y'all was hitting," Laconia said.

She and Jock thought that was the funniest shit they'd ever heard before, because they laughed themselves into tears. Rika and Boogie, on the other hand didn't find it so funny (but the thought sure sounded nice).

Boogie looked at her and motioned with his lips, "Not a bad idea." Rika looked at him and simply smiled. Just the thought of that idea sent waves through her.

"Rika, you know what's up. Don't act like you all shy and shit. You know my folks been trying to pop at you for some time now, and all he keep getting is the cold shoulder," Jock said.

Jock was so caught up in the moment, that he didn't even notice Laconia when she took the joint out of his hand and fired it up.

"Thanks, Jock, for talking so much. Now, do you want to smoke or what? And, for the record, get you some business and stay out of theirs. I'm sure if Rika and Boogie wanted to hook up they don't need a boy cheerleader," Laconia said.

"I know that's right. And, by the way, while you all in mine, when you gone let Laconia know that you got a thing for her? Or are you just going to keep inviting her over to smoke up your weed and watch her like you are some kind of pervert?"

Now, the whole house was turned upside-down in laughter. Rika don't think Jock wanted Laconia to know all that because, if he was any lighter, he would have been beet red.

"What's wrong? Cat got your tongue? And by the way, Boogie don't find me attractive. We are just friends."

"Woa! Hold up. You can't speak for me. How do you know what I feel? And by the way, I am attracted to you. I'm just waiting for the perfect time to make my move, and it seems like today is your day."

He winked at her and took a drink of his beer. *Wow*, was all Rika could think. The truth was, she was physically attracted to him but, spiritually and emotionally, she really wasn't. She was too young to know the difference. One thing Rika did know was that you shouldn't heat the oven if you're not going to put nothing in it. So, she followed that physical part of herself.

"Ay, Rika, come holla at me in the other room so we can let these clowns keep getting high and laugh at each other," Boogie said.

On that note, Rika got up and followed Boogie to the other room. When she first walked in the room, all she noticed all over the wall was a bunch of those old nasty ass posters with different girls on them. Rika thought to herself, *He must jack-off to this bullshit at night*. That thought alone turned her off big time. There was a king-sized bed with just a sheet and a comforter spread across the foot of the bed. He had what looked like a 19" TV on the top of the dresser, with a clothes hanger hanging out of the back of it.

Clothes were all shoved in the corner, apparently needing to be washed. Her mother would have had a fit if they kept their room in the shape that this room was in. In spite of the mess, she was ready to see what all the fuss was about. She was tired of being secretly teased because she hadn't had sex. *Besides, I look good, I dress nice. Why not have somebody like Boogie on my team?*

"Rika, are you ready to step this up a notch?" He asked, taking off his shirt.

"Looks like I don't have a choice. Now, do I?"

"Yeah, you have a choice. I just hope you choose the right one. I know that you are a virgin. So, I'll be gentle," he said, smiling and locking the door at the same time.

"Well, if I have a choice, then why are you locking the door before I give you my answer?"

The truth was, she had already made up her mind. This was it. Rika was ready for some big girl stuff. She just didn't know that this one mistake would come back and bite her so hard that nobody but God could save her.

"Come here let me touch your soft ass body."

Reaching his hands out for her to grab, when she did, it was all she wrote. She was so caught up in the moment that she didn't even bother to ask if he had on a rubber. *It didn't matter*, Rika thought. She still couldn't tell you what happened. She thought she blacked out from time to time. She kept thinking to herself, *This shit don't feel good at all. Is this what all the fuss is about? Well they can keep this shit.* All of a sudden, she felt him going faster and faster, then he collapsed on top of her.

Rika laid there, looking confused. She didn't know whether to push him off her or lie there with him still inside of her. Well, of course, she chose option number one. She told him to, "Get the hell off me." She couldn't bare the thought of him another second. She got dressed and headed towards the door and never looked back.

Four months passed since Rika experimented with the whole sex thing. Boogie and she had crossed each other's paths a time or two, but nothing really major. Over those few months, her body had changed tremendously. Her breasts were bigger than ever, her stomach was starting to protrude through all of her clothes, and her mother was starting to become very suspicious. All Rika remembered was one minute she was going to the doctor to see if she was pregnant and, the next thing she knew, the house was packed up and they were California bound.

REFLECTIONS

First, let me take this opportunity to say, "Thank you for getting this far with this novel." When God first put the thought to write this book in my heart, I was very hesitant. He always gives me challenges that are far beyond my wildest dreams. It was a year prior to me even attempting sitting down and typing my first letter of this book. He had to start a fire in me for me to even get the concept of how important it was for me to give birth to this assignment.

No matter where you are in your life, God has a purpose and plan for you -- whether you believe it or not. You may not even see it for yourself or, if it's a thought that continues to run around in your head from time to time, there is someone around you that can see that fire burning deep inside of you. No, not all the time do we know right off if it's really God speaking to us. But, I can guarantee, He has placed someone or something in your life to assure you that He is real and you're not crazy. When He gives us challenges, we are already equipped to do the job. That's why the fire burns within us to do things that the opposition has no clue about.

God may have told you to write a book, or to help your neighbor with their children to prepare you for your own. Not to mention the time He may have told you to keep your house cleaned because maybe He was getting you ready for your spouse. This goes for you men too. What about the fire that He set in you to stop crying and start praying? It's not a coincident that you have this book in your hands right now. This is not for everyone to read.

At first, I questioned the fact of having these types of reflections in the course of this kind of book. Well, of course. God had to let me see things His way, and this is how I understood it. If you are walking down the street, and you just so happen to look down and see a twenty-dollar bill sort of buried in the dirt, would you walk past it?

Of course you wouldn't. So, imagine this one. What if you were walking up to a friend's car and you looked down and saw a hundred-dollar bill buried in some dog poop? Would you walk right by it? Or, would you find a stick and scrape the poop off enough for you to get a nice grip on it so you can wipe it off?

Well, that's what He wants for you to do with this book. Treat it like a hundred-dollar bill buried in poop. Why not find treasures in the dirt? Sometimes, in life, we also cause our own spiritual fires and natural fires. So, since we all have an understanding of what fire is and what it can do, I ask you this question: "What's the fire that consumes you?"

Chapter Four

On the outside, Showboat seemed to be the happiest kid alive. But, deep down inside, there was something missing he still couldn't figure it out. One would think that, since now he was living with his mom, it would fill that empty void in his life. But, for some reason, he was still sad and unhappy. Months had gone by since he had moved to Topeka, and he had started making friends. Of course, he made a couple of bad choices -- one being an older White woman, who happened to be a friend of his mom.

Karla was one of the baddest White bitches Showboat had ever seen, not to mention that she was older and she had money. Karla stood five feet easy, with long jet-black hair. She seemed to have a year-round tan and, for a White girl, she had ass for days. Often, she would come over and buy Showboat all kinds of things that were considered to be friendly gifts. But you can best believe that Pat was no fool. One day she pulled Showboat to the side and asked him was something going on with him and Karla, and of course he lied.

"If I find out you fucking that bitch, it's gonna be hell to tell the captain," Pat screamed!

"It ain't even like dat. She's your friend, so that makes her my friend, right?"

Pat knew he was full of shit. But, that was her baby so what he said was law, period. Pat worked for a physical fitness center and often times she would work long hours just to make things a little easier for her son and her. She would come home and have to cook dinner, and that was something she wasn't use to so they ate out lot. One night, she came in late from work and Showboat had one of his buddies over.

"Hi, boys. What are y'all doing up so late? Have y'all ate anything?"

"Yeah. Karla ordered us some pizza, and she said she was going to call you in the morning cause she want you to take her to handle some business," Showboat said to his mother in a baby voice.

Now, Pat couldn't quite get the full picture, but she smelled a rat. And, she was going to get to the bottom of this shit, even if it cost her a trip back to those familiar walls. Early the next morning, she got up and showered, left twenty dollars on the dresser like she always did, grabbed her purse, and headed towards the door when Showboat startled her.

"Moms, where you going so early this morning?"

"I'm going to pick up Karla and run some errands. I'll be back. And, when you start questioning me about my whereabouts? By the way, what you doing up so early on a Saturday morning?"

"I don't know, I just can't sleep. I been thinking about grandma all night and, well, I don't know, I kinda miss her. Do you think that's strange?" He said with tears in his eyes.

"Look, I miss her too, but I try not to think about it cause it'll just make things worse for me. Now, you go in there and get you some breakfast and I'll be back in a little while. And, try not to think so much, okay."

With that, Pat turned around and, in seconds, she was gone. Showboat did just what she said – except, instead of going to the kitchen to get him some breakfast, he headed to the phone to call Kameisha.

"Hey, baby. Were you sleep?" He asked.

"No, just laying here thinking about you. Why didn't you call me back last night?" Kameisha asked.

"My mom came home early last night," he lied.

The truth was, he had Karla come over and give him the magic brain service that she did so well. And, for some reason, he couldn't understand why she was giving him the royal treatment when she knew he was only fourteen. Showboat enjoyed playing in Karla's twat. In fact, no girl has ever let him do the things to theirs that Karla lets him do to hers. She even lets him stick four fingers inside of her, and from there it went to toys and so forth and so on.

"Well, you know my momma got her phone bill. Now, I am grounded for a whole month. And she beat my ass for it! But, for you, it's all worth it," Kameisha said.

Kameisha had mastered the game of stroking his ego and she knew just what to say and when to say it. Little did Showboat know, she had a few secret of her own and wasn't the sweet little angel that he once knew.

"I can't wait to see you again so we can be together. I hate it here, but don't worry. And, I don't think my mom is feeling this whole mother thing, so I'll be back. I don't know when or how, but I know," Showboat said.

"Yeah, I know, but don't get yourself into any trouble though. I am waiting."

They talked for a few more minutes and said their I-Love-Yous and hung up the phone. Showboat awoke his homeboy so they could get ready and hit the streets. But, they were stopped dead in their tracks when the door swung open.

"I'm about to beat the shit out of you, you little muthafucka," Pat yelled.

From the looks of things, Showboat thought he saw fire shoot from her ears. Following close behind her was Karla, shaking like a whore in church.

"Moms, hold up. What is going on? I can explain," he said.

The young boy hadn't seen Pat this upset since she and Felicia were fighting over a pair of shoes.

"You can't explain shit! What the hell were you thinking, running my fucking bill up to $600? And, on top of that, you tried to hide it from me. That little bitch, Kameisha, just cost you a royal ass kicking."

At first, he stood there speechless. But, before he could think of a lie to tell, Karla butted in.

"Who were you talking to?" She asked with an evil glare in her eyes.

"Kameisha," Pat said, never taking her eyes off Showboat.

In the back of Pat's mind, she couldn't help but to think: *What does it matter who he was talking to*, when her bill was $600 and, *Who was going to pay it?* Plus, something still seemed a little strange. *Was this bitch sitting in my face and fucking my young son? If that is the case, I'm about to kill two birds with one stone.* With that, an even better idea came to mind.

"Why do it matter who he was talking to?" Pat asked aloud.

"I was just under the impression that he didn't talk to the bitch!" Karla spat.

Showboat forgot that he lied and told her that he didn't talk to Kameisha anymore, and that was the only reason she did the things she did for him in the first place.

"Listen, I can explain, I\"

Before anything else came out of his mouth, Pat slapped fire out of him.

"Now I'm going to ask you one more time," Pat said.

"I'll pay the bill," Karla said through her teeth.

"Why in the fuck do you want to pay a bill that this little 14-year-old boy ran up? And for the record, are you fucking my son?"

Showboat felt like he was going to pass out. *I hope this bitch don't be stupid, and get us both killed.*

"Yes, I am, and I think I'm in love with him, so if it\"

That was all she wrote. Pat commenced to kicking the lining out of her ass. All you saw was legs, arms and blood. Showboat thought this was the perfect time to make his escape. He looked at his homeboy and with that, they broke for the door. When he had made it almost to the end of the block, all he heard was tires screeching. When he looked back, all he saw was Pat rolling on the curb trying to run his ass over. If it wasn't for his friend, Josh, pulling him out of the way, she would have run him over.

"I'mma kill your little Black ass," Pat screamed from the driver side window.

"This bitch done lost her mind for real. I gotta get the fuck up outta here," Showboat told Josh.

By the time he made it to his friend's house, Showboat was out of breath. He sat down for a few minutes before he asked to use the phone. Josh handed him the phone. Showboat was so nervous that he could barely dial the number. He finally pulled himself together. Flint picked up on the first ring.

"Yo, yo," Flint answered.

"Hey Pops! What you doing?" Showboat asked, sniffling.

Flint could tell something was wrong and that his son had been crying.

"What's up, Bubba? Why are you crying?"

"Man, she's crazy!"

Flint didn't even have to ask whom Showboat was talking about, because he had his fair share of fistfights with Pat. He remembered times he had to pull her off of chicks at the club. She was no punk when it came to fighting. All Flint wanted to know was where to pick up his son. The last time he heard from Showboat was when Showboat was living in Kansas City with Felicia.

"She tried to run me over with her car!"

Flint didn't even bother to ask what he had done to make her that mad. And, furthermore, he didn't care. All he knew was that Pat went too far this time, and he was coming to take his son no matter what she said.

"Where are you?"

"Over my friend Josh's house."

"I'm on my way now. Let me speak to one of his parents, preferably his dad."

Showboat handed the phone to Josh's step-father, Jesse. Just like Showboat, Josh wanted to go live with his father but his mother wouldn't let him. Josh was a troubled child too. At the age of nine, his parents got a divorce and his mother was awarded custody of him. He had been going to an alternative school since he was in the fifth grade because he beat a boy with his chair.

After Jesse hung up the phone with Flint, he went in the kitchen and told Katherine about the arrangements. By the time Flint arrived, Showboat was sitting on the front porch waiting. As soon as he saw the 98 drop-top hit the corner, Showboat had a smile as wide as the freeway all across his face. Flint parked, jumped out of the car, and headed straight towards his son.

"Hey, Bubba! I see you still sit on the porch and wait for me to scoop you up," he said as he grabbed him and gave him a big hug.

This was one of the happiest days for Flint and Showboat. Flint finally got to take his son with him, and Showboat got his wish.

"Yeah, you know it," Showboat said while smiling at his hero.

"Go say hello to Precious, and wait for me so we can go get your stuff."

Showboat went and sat in the car like his dad had told him to do. He and Precious made small talk until Flint came back to the car. Precious was Flint's woman and soon-to-be wife. They had been seeing each other for several years now. Precious had two sons, Calvin and Eddie, who were around the same age as Showboat. Her daughter named Nesha was nine years old.

Precious was extremely short with dark skin and a body that would put a horse to rest. She wasn't the rowdy type that Flint was use to dating, but she would handle her business if a challenge came her way. She was the mother that Showboat never had, and Flint knew that. That's why he didn't mind bringing him home with them.

When Flint got in the car the first thing he said was, "Where do you live? And listen, when we get there, don't get out of the car until I tell you to. You hear me?" He asked, looking at Showboat in his rearview mirror.

"Yeah," Showboat answered with a strange look on his face.

That comment even caught Precious's attention. She looked at him for a split second and turned her gaze back out of her window. She knew better than to question any of Flint's decisions, especially when it came to his son. When they pulled up to Pat's house, her car was parked across the grass as if she was in a rush or something.

Flint stepped out of the car and went up the four steps it took to get to the front door, and he began to knock. Pat came to the door in a white see-through gown, wearing some white fur slippers. As soon as she saw Flint, she opened the door and headed back to sit down on the couch. She grabbed her cigarettes off the coffee table, took one out of the pack with her lips, and lit it.

She looked up at Flint, looking fine as ever, and said, "So what brings you here?"

"Don't play no fucking games with me! I'm here to get his shit, and I'm taking him back with me," Flint told her.

"You not taking my son nowhere! All of a sudden, you want to step in and play daddy? I don't think so! And furthermore, did he tell you what the hell he did?" Pat asked.

Flint didn't answer at first. He was too busy looking at all the blood on the walls. From the looks of it, Pat had tried to clean it off, but she forgot some spots. The thing that puzzled Flint was that Showboat didn't look like he took that kind of ass kicking. *What the hell really happened here?* Now, that's what made him stay concrete to his word that he was taking his son.

"I don't care what he done. All I care about is his safety," he finally answered, still looking at the walls and down at the floor.

"Well, all I know is you're not taking him nowhere, so you might as well get your something-like-a-pimp ass up outta here before we go to war," Pat said.

She took another drag off of her cigarette, and was stunned when she couldn't breathe. She didn't even see it coming. Flint had her around the neck before she knew it.

"I'm taking my son whether you like it or not. Now, I'm tired of you telling me when and how to be a father. I put up with that shit when your momma was living, Lord rest her soul, but you, you I'll kill. Now, tell me where his shit is so I can get the fuck outta here," Flint snapped back.

When he heard her gasp for air, he stepped away nice and slow. He was no stranger to Pat at all. He knew she wasn't going to take that shit lightly. As soon as he stepped back far enough, she charged his ass.

"Fuck you, bitch! You bet not ever put your hands on me, nigga! I hate you!"

Flint stopped dead in his tracks when he felt blood come from his lip.

"You crazy bitch," he shouted as he grabbed her by her neck and threw her to the ground.

Flint was known for carrying an ice pick. Somehow, he managed to pull it out of his lime green gator low cut boot. He put it in Pat's side. As soon as she felt the tip of it, she stopped fighting.

He got right in her ear and whispered, "You better listen, and listen good. I'm leaving with my son and there's nothing you can do to stop me.

Now, you can tell me where his shit is, or you can keep it. Either way, he's going. Now, I didn't come here to fight with you, so when I let you up, you bet not try nothing because I would hate for my son to watch them bury his mother. And, by the way, you smell good."

As he was getting off of her, he licked the side of her face. Just as he was putting the ice pick back in his boot, he looked up and saw Showboat.

Chapter Five

It was about a two-hour drive back to Wichita, and Showboat had some mixed emotions. He was still curious about what he saw when he walked into the house. To him, it looked like they were having sex -- that is, until his daddy got up and Showboat noticed the blood coming from Flint's lip and he was putting something in his boot. Even though Pat and Flint said everything was fine, Showboat knew that it wasn't. While he was sitting in the car, he heard all of the commotion. He was sure Precious heard the same thing but she just sat there like she didn't hear a thing.

One thing about Pat she stayed hot so she would always leave her windows open to let some fresh air in. As he sat in the backseat staring out of the window, Showboat wondered what would happen to Pat now that he was gone. She needed him there to protect her from her crazy boyfriend. But, he knew that she would eventually kill him or he would be in jail for a long time if he stayed.

He remembered the time he got mad at Pat and kicked a big dent in her car. She didn't notice it until the night her and her boyfriend L'Roy and came back from the club drunk and she staggered out of the car and noticed the dent.

"Muthafucka, you done wrecked my car," she yelled, slurring every word.

"What the fuck you talking about? I ain't wrecked shit! Now, come on and get your drunk ass in the house before you wake up the neighbors with that bullshit," L'Roy said, walking on the other side of the car to see what she was talking about.

"I ain't going nowhere until you tell me how you wrecked my car, and had the nerve to not say shit," Pat screamed.

L'Roy squinted to see the dent she was talking about. Sure enough, it was as big as the day.

"I didn't do it. It wasn't me. Maybe it was your other nigga," he said in a drunken voice.

"Hell naw! You did that shit!"

Pat tried to swing at him, but she missed. She was moving in slow motion. He finally helped her in the house. He had her on one arm, and his glass that he took from the club in the other. They continued to argue until they woke up Showboat. He came out of the room rubbing his eyes when all he saw was L'Roy push his mom, and that's when Showboat went to work on L'Roy's ass.

When Pat saw how fast he attacked his ass, she sobered up real quick and they tag-teamed his ass. L'Roy broke the glass he had from the club, and cut Showboat across his neck. When Pat saw blood coming from his neck, she blacked out and almost killed him. Showboat picked him up and threw him down the steps, and he was out for the count.

Pat dragged her son in the house and closed the door. Once they were inside the house, she looked at his neck still bleeding. She panicked, and rushed him to the hospital. The doctor said if it had been a half inch closer, he would have died.

Showboat didn't realize they were pulling up in front of his father's house until he felt the bump from them pulling into the drive way. That's when he knew this was it, there had to be something better for him in life. So far, life was giving him lemons and nobody taught him how to make lemonade. He sat there for a few minutes after he heard his Pops turn off the ignition, just gazing out the window looking at the yard his father had worked so hard to maintain.

"Oh. So, I guess you are going to live in the car now, uhh? Come on son, get out the car. Everything is going to be alright now. You're safe, so don't worry about nothing. I know you've been through a lot, so I'm going to make it my business to see to it that life goes a little bit smoother for you from here on out."

Showboat gazed deeply into his father's eyes, looking for some sort of comfort. Let the truth be told, he didn't find any. He wanted to cry so badly. But, he learned at an early age that "a man ain't supposed to cry!" So, Showboat picked up enough strength to get out of the car and walked towards the house with his daddy right behind him.

Flint didn't understand. Wasn't this what he always wanted? *Damn.* Flint didn't know what to do to make his son feel better. *Will I be a good dad to him?* For starters, his son was turning into a man and Flint didn't even know him anymore. *What do teenagers like to do? I know what I was doing at the age of fourteen.* That thought quickly vanished.

Flint knew when he was fourteen, his was a life of money, sex and violence, and he sent his father through hell. But Flint wanted something different for his son. *What could that be?* Flint brushed off all of those thoughts because they made him think too much. *I know what I can do! I'll take him shopping. Yeah, that always work. And, besides, I did leave all his shit in Topeka. Yeah, that's it.*

The truth of the matter was, that was all Flint knew to do, but what Showboat really needed was love. When they walked in to the house, Precious was headed into their room. The house was nice. It had the cave man ceilings that Flint had custom made, and the living room was nice with a baby blue sectional and the end tables to match. On the walls were all kinds of family portraits of everyone from friends and family to Showboat and Flint in their leather and mink coats Flint ordered out of a catalog in Chicago. The kitchen sat off the side where the dining room was. Downstairs was the basement that they had fixed up, and there were two bedrooms and a bathroom that had been set up for the older boys.

Showboat walked in and was greeted by his two step-brothers (Calvin and Eddie) and his little sister, Nesha. Now Nesha was Flint's little princess, and he could count on her to keep him up on all the things that were going on when he would leave the house for days at a time. In other words, she was his informant.

"Hi, brother! I missed you. Are you moving in with us?" She asked, giving him one of the biggest hugs a girl her age could give.

"Yeah," Showboat said, trying to put on a fake smile.

He really wasn't feeling all this just yet because that wasn't his family, even though he was no stranger to them at all. He just wanted things to be like they used to be at his grandmother's house.

Flint went into the kitchen where Precious was starting to prepare for dinner. He could tell she had an attitude, so he just simply kissed her on the forehead and told her he would be back shortly.

She looked up at him with fire in her eyes and said, "Oh, just like that, you gone just leave? Don't you think we need to talk about what happened up there with you and Pat?"

"Not now baby, I need to catch the mall before it close," Flint said.

Precious knew that was a crock of shit. *Hell, it's only 5:30 in the afternoon, and the mall don't close until 9:00.*

"So you think I'm some kind of fool now, uhh Flint?" Precious asked.

"Not now, short stuff. We can talk when I come back. And make sure you make the boy some potatoes. You know that's his favorite."

Precious just stood there looking at him. *Hell, I know what the boy like because I was the one he came to when he was hungry.*

"I know," she said. "And while you're at the mall, pick the boys up some more socks and Nesha need some new shoes."

After that was said, Precious turned back around and finished what she was doing. She didn't like it too much when Flint would leave like that. She had almost forgotten the feeling she had when Showboat was around. She knew that Flint had a special bond with him, and this was all he wanted, he and his son.

"Com'on boy. Let's get you to the mall so I can get you ready for school tomorrow."

Flint winked at his son and off they went to Towne East Mall. Showboat got all kinds of stuff, from shoes to earrings. You name it, Flint bought it. Anything for his boy! They even stopped at the food court and got ice cream. The shopping got so good that Flint forgot all about the things that Precious told him to get for the other kids.

On the ride home, Flint stopped at one of his lady friend's house to introduce her to his son. When they pulled up to Georgia's house, Flint motioned for Showboat to get out of the car. Now, Flint didn't have to school him not to mention this to Precious because he already knew what time it was. Before they even made it to the front door, Georgia opened it.

"Hey, baby!"

She embraced him with some love, Flint returned the love right back. Georgia wore a long black wig that hung past her shoulders, with the china bangs. She was about a half inch shorter than Flint with ass for days to be an older woman. Her skin was clear with a honey tint; the only thing that threw her off was she wore those fake eyelashes and too much damn make-up. Before she closed the door, Flint smacked her on the ass, as always. Only this time, it startled her a bit.

"Not in front of the boy," Georgia said with a naughty little grin.

"Who? Him? This ain't no boy, this is my little man. I brought him over to meet you. Georgia, this is Bentley Junior. And, Bentley, this is Georgia."

"Nice to meet you," she said extending her hand.

"Nice to meet you too," Showboat replied.

"Lattice, come here. I have someone I want you to meet," she yelled into the other room.

All of the sudden, out of the room emerged a beautiful young girl who looked to be about fifteen. She was wearing some black biker shorts with the half top to match. She had pretty skin as well. She stood 5'6" easy, her thighs were thick, and her legs were a bronze color to match her skin. She had the deepest dimples Showboat had ever seen.

Showboat was speechless. He hadn't seen no one this fine since Kameisha. They introduced Lattice and Showboat to each other, then Flint and Georgia disappeared in the other room and left them in the living room.

"Wait, let me turn my TV off," Lattice said.

Showboat sat there in his own thoughts. *Damn, Pops sure know how to pick 'em. Damn, her daughter is fine. I wonder if she has a man? Shit, I don't give a fuck. She's about to be my girl.* His thoughts were interrupted with the thought of Kameisha. *Damn I haven't even called her since I been here. Oh well, I'll just sit back for a few days and see what's really going on.* Lattice came back in and sat down on the other couch that sat across from him.

"I didn't know Flint had a son. Where do you go to school?"

"Well, to answer your first question, I'm his only son, and I just got back from Topeka. As far as school, I don't know yet, but I think I will be going to Wilbur. Why? What school do you go to?"

"Coleman," she said, trying to seem bored with the conversation.

Showboat sensed that, so he changed the subject. "Can I have some water?"

Knowing that he wasn't thirsty, he just wanted her to get up and walk so he could see her ass in those tight ass shorts. When she went into the kitchen to get him some water, that gave him a chance to regroup and hit her with some of his charm. She re-entered the room with a glass of red Kool-Aid.

"I figured you wanted some ghetto punch instead. I made it myself," she said and they both fell out laughing.

That broke the ice. He didn't even have to go in for the kill, because she did it for him.

"Do you have a girlfriend yet?"

"Damn, girl. Didn't I tell you I just got here? What's it to you anyway?"

"I'm just asking, smart ass. I'm just trying to help you out."

"Okay, how is that helping me out? I'm not looking for a girlfriend right now. I'm just taking it slow. Girls are bad news."

"Maybe the ones you mess with. That's why you need to find yourself a young lady," she said, hoping he would catch the hint.

"How can you say that? You don't even know nothing about me or the girls I go out with," Showboat responded.

"I'm just saying."

"So, do you consider yourself a young lady?" He asked, leaning in closer to hear her response.

"Yeah," Lattice shot back with a confident look on her face.

"Well, let me be the judge of that. Now, first of all, how old are you?" He asked, leaning back on the couch crossing his hands over his chest.

"Fourteen, and how old are you?" She responded, leaning back on the couch mocking him with a smirk on her face.

"Slow your roll, I'm asking the questions. Now, do you get good grades in school?" He said, turning his top lip up.

"If you consider A's and B's good, then yeap!"

"Mmmm, do you dress like that to go to school?" Showboat asked, pointing at Lattice's shorts.

"What's wrong with my shorts?" She asked and let out a sigh.

Now, he was starting to offend her. Showboat knew exactly what he was doing.

"Well, the young ladies that I know don't wear stuff like that, only hood-rats wear that kind of stuff. So maybe you should think about what you want to be, now which is it?"

Now, he was really pushing her buttons, but she wasn't going to let him see her sweat. Little did he know, she was used to guys like him. The truth of the matter was, she was very intelligent and she was a top player on the basketball team. Lattice also played the piano and she could sing. The only thing that threw her off was the boys thought she was too Black and they would tease her and call her names like "Midnight" and "Tar Baby." Even though he was offending her, she liked the fact that he never made her skin complexion an issue. She sat there for a few minutes, thinking of a comeback, and then finally she spoke.

"I see you're not so bright, because it's not what you wear it's how you wear it. Second of all, when you wear stuff like this, you don't wear it outside, it's in-house only. Now, what do you have to say?"

Showboat sat there in silence. He couldn't say anything. She had him. What she was saying was true, but he wouldn't have known that had he never asked. But since they were on the subject of hood-rats, it was time to set in for the kill.

"Have you ever had sex?" He asked.

Lattice never changed her expression, but she was kind of stunned. The closest she had ever come to sex was when she would please herself in the shower.

"Wouldn't you like to know, uhh? I don't think that's any of you business," Lattice said.

She started laughing so hard until she had tears in her eyes. He even had to laugh himself. They were still laughing when Flint and Georgia entered the room.

"I see they hit it off just fine," Georgia whispered in Flint's ear.

Flint looked at his son with a proud look on his face. He hadn't seen him laugh like that in a long time.

"Let's go, son," he said.

Everyone said their good-byes, and, off Flint and Showboat went.

Chapter Six

By the time Rika's family made it to California, the sun was just starting to come up over those big palm trees. The only people who were on the streets were the people going to work and the travelers. It was a Saturday morning. The air was full of pollution, but it was so much different from where they came from. Texarkana had more trees, and it was a little country town compared to Los Angeles. But, this was Rika's real home. Her mother moved the family down south when she was about nine years old.

Roslyn had moved the family to Texas four years earlier to give them a fresh start and explore new options. Roslyn, also known as Queen, was a mother of five. But, when she left California, she only took her three youngest children with her. The two oldest wanted to stay for whatever reason. She agreed to leave them with her grandmother, Grandma Katherine, which she regretted later.

During the time she was in Texas, her only son was murdered at a movie theater in L.A. Some guys tried to rob him for his leather jacket. He was stabbed and pronounced DOA. Even though it was their choice to stay there, her oldest daughter, Camille, blamed Queen for his death. She felt like Queen showed favoritism toward her light-skinned kids, and treated the darker ones differently. Queen was a praying woman, and she believed in the Bible with all she had in her. The real truth was, she didn't have any favorites. When her children were much younger, she would pray over all their lives.

Being a single mother, she had to go to God for some directions. She asked God to show her each one of her kids' characters, and, because He is so faithful, He did. Now, no one understood her choices, so she spent a lot of her life being the villain -- which was another reason she moved her children away from the family. They thought she put her kids on a pedestal, and often they would say things like, "Let me hold Little Jesus."

They didn't understand that her kids were her life, and that's what kept her breathing. Without them, she would have thrown in the towel along time ago. A few months before she decided to move back, Queen's middle daughter (Justine) moved back home, and was staying with Queen's sister. Justine was a troubled teen. A few months after her brother got killed, she tried to commit suicide and almost succeeded.

They pulled up in front of her sister's house, and Queen just sat there for a few minutes to collect her thoughts. She was a little frustrated, being that there she was once again back in California after she vowed never to return.

"Listen to me! When we go in here, keep your mouth shut. You hear me? We're only going to be here until we find us a place to live. I don't have a whole lot of money, but we're going to do the best we can," Queen said. "Rika, I don't want no shit outta you. Rodge, I want you to make sure all the trash gets taken out every morning, and, Rika, you make sure our clothes stay in one spot. You're pregnant, not handicap, so don't pull that bull. This is not our house, so we may have to endure some hardship but we'll make it with God's help."

Rika knew her mother meant business and she wasn't taking no shit. So, she and her brother kicked into fifth gear and stuck together like they always did to help momma out. Rodge was the baby boy. Rika looked up to him because he was the only male figure she had in her life for a while. They got out of the car, walked up to the door, and waited for Aunt Hope to answer. She came to the door wearing what looked like a sheet.

"Hey girl, I thought you would never make it. What happened? Did you get lost or something?" She said, showing all twenty-eight teeth

"Come give me a hug, Rika, with yo' fast ass -- pregnant at the age of thirteen. I should kick yo' ass. Hey, Rodge, baby. Come give auntie a hug."

"Where's everybody at?" Rika asked, trying to get far out of her sight.

"They in the room go back there. See if they woke!"

Still all smiles, she didn't have to tell her twice. The house was so big, Rika didn't know which room she was talking about. The first room she went in, her uncle was sprawled out all over some white lady that she had never seen before. At the foot of the bed was a little boy with his hair all over his head who looked like he was mixed. So, she closed the door back very slow. The next room must have been one of her cousin's. She could tell from all the posters that were on the walls of different magazines.

Finally, Rika came to a room that sat in the far back of the house. From the looks of it, they must have added it on because you had to walk up some steps. She opened the door and there they were, watching television. All at once, they turned, looked and started screaming and hollering. They hadn't seen each other since Rika's brother's funeral.

"What's up, Rika? Damn, you got a little pooch. Where's your stuff?" Her cousin, Carima, had the questions rolling.

Carima was one of her older cousins, and she still treated her like a baby. Unlike all the rest of the family, Carima and Rika had some sort of connection. When Rika looked over her shoulder to see who was sitting on Carima's bed not looking in their direction, she couldn't believe it. It was her sister, Justine. *Damn, ain't she going to speak?* So, Rika decided to speak to her.

"Hi, Justine," she said.

Justine turned slightly and mumbled. Rika could tell by the tone in her voice she really didn't want to say anything. She took the hint and kept talking to her other cousins. Rodge wasn't having that shit. He just flat out asked her:

"Oh, you not speaking? So it's like that?" He was standing directly in front of the television Justine was watching.

"Hell naw, now get the fuck from in front of the TV!"

"Okay. You remember that," he said and didn't say another word.

Rodge wasn't with all the drama. He felt like we're family and they should let bygones be bygones. Justine always had problems. Every time you turn around, she had an attitude about something. From day-to-day, you never knew what to think about her. But, every since Rika was a little girl, Justine didn't like her. Because she was the baby, her mother used to let her get away with so much, so Justine harbored these feelings deep down inside. Every now and then, her true colors would show just how much she really hated Rika. Over the years, she proved just how much.

Over the next few months, things had gotten hectic. They were living from Rika's aunt's house to her grandmother's to her great-grandmother's house. Once, Rika's mother thought she had found a house for them. Then, come to find out, the man she gave her deposit to wasn't even the owner. He was just someone the owner hired to paint the house. So, now she was out of money and had no house. Queen wasn't a pushover. She knew how to hustle and was good at it. But, this wasn't what she wanted to do. So, she had to start all over again. *Back to the drawing board.*

"Finally," she said, as she was dropping them off at school. "'The Lord has blessed us with our own place. It's off of 82nd & Hooper. It's not all that big, but it's ours. Rodge, you have to sleep in the living room for a while so Rika and the baby can have their own room."

They didn't care, as long as they had their own place.

"Thank you Jesus! When can we go see it?" Rika said, giving Rodge a high five.

"Today when I pick you up from school. And ya'll know how I feel when God bless us don't\" and before she could finish her sentence, they did it for her, "/don't tell nobody."

They all had a good laugh. It had been a long time since Rika saw her mother smile. She had been under so much stress lately. Rika knew this was a big relief for her -- from hospitals to house hunting and getting ripped off, all the way down to her husband getting tired of waiting to be with his family. It all finally paid off, and they were now moving into their very own place.

It was the last class of the day, and time couldn't go by fast enough. It had been a long time since they had their own space. All Rika kept thinking about was bringing her baby home and fixing up her new room. Even though she didn't know how to pray, Rika just kept saying, "Thank you Jesus," every time she thought about it.

It was now three o'clock and the bell had just rung. Rika didn't have much homework, so her books were light. The teacher was still talking when Rika sprinted out the door and down the hallway. She was one of the first kids standing out waiting to be picked up. She looked to her left and then to her right. There were no signs of her mom or Rodge.

Rika was just about to go sit down when she heard Rodge scream her name. On the way to their new house, you could just feel all the excitement and faith that filled the car. They talked and played non-stop. When they pulled up to the tiny duplex, her heart stopped. It was nothing like she had expected. It was a total nightmare!

Rodge spoke first, "Oh my God. Moms, what are we suppose to do with this?"

"We have to do some painting and lawn work, and plug up a few holes, but it's ours. You know, by the time I'm done, it will look and feel like a mansion."

They both knew she wasn't lying. They decided to get out of the car. The grass was a hot mess. It looked like nobody had lived here for years. The place was a light tan with what looked like burgundy trim. Some of the cement on the front steps needed to be repaired. Queen turned the key, and they all walked in as if they were waiting for something to jump out at them. To Rika's surprise, it wasn't as bad as it looked on the outside. Queen was right. All they had to do was patch up a few holes and do some painting, and they were in there.

Rodge looked over at her and they both began to sing, "We got our own house! We got our own house!"

That was a big relief for Queen. They had approved her findings.

"When can we start painting and fixing up the place?" Rodge asked.

"Willie C is sending us some money in the morning. So, while you guys are at school, I will go and get all the supplies. We have to move quick because Nila will be home soon."

"Why do we have to go to school? The sooner we get this task out of the way, the quicker we can move in. I don't have no test tomorrow. How about you, Rika?"

She was in her own world looking all around the tiny space. "No," she screamed from the other room.

"Do you want to stay home from school and help Mama paint and get the house ready?"

"Sure, no problem."

"Now hold on a minute before ya'll go making plans. Your Aunt Hope has some business to take care of in the morning. So, we will pick ya'll up after school."

Rika and Rodge looked at each other. They knew anytime Queen and Hope got together something was about to go down. Hope was Rika's favorite aunt, and she and her mom were really close. Rika loved her because she kept it real. Hope was a dark version of her mom. They had smiles that would light up the night and tempers that could assassinate the president. They knew not to ask any questions, just trust what was said.

The next day, when Queen came to pick them up, the car was loaded down with all kinds of stuff -- from gallons of paint to sheet rock, to bags and bags of other stuff. That's when Rika knew this wasn't going to be an easy task.

"Rika, we're dropping you off at the hospital for a few hours so we can take this stuff to the house. Make sure you ask the doctor when they are going to release her."

They pulled up to the hospital and Rika jumped out. She walked in and went up to the seventh floor to check-in. As usual, she had to scrub her hands for five minutes and put on a gown over her clothes. As she began to walk down the hall to the nursery where her baby was, she was stopped by one of the nurses.

"Hello there, Ms. Rika. Did your mom come with you today?"

Rika smiled and said, "No. Why? Is there something wrong?

"Well, I talked with Dr. Daruso and he's wanting to release your baby girl sometime this week. She's doing really well. I also have some papers for you to fill out."

"What kind of papers?"

"Just some release forms. It's normal when it's almost time for babies to go home. Aren't you excited?"

"Of course!"

"Me too. I know you are going to be a good mother, and you have a lot of support."

Rika knew she really didn't mean it. Since her baby had been on this floor, her mama had been giving their ass the blues. Rika said goodbye and went to see her daughter. When she picked her up, Nila smiled at her. That was the first time she ever did that. Rika's heart was filled with faith. That was when she knew everything was going to be okay.

Visiting hours were over, and Rika walked out of the hospital feeling like a real mom. Nobody could take that feeling away from her. With all the criticism she had endured, all the tears she had shed, after seeing Nila smile at her, it was all worth it. *Now, I know what it really feels like to be a proud parent.*

Over the next six months, things had changed tremendously. Rodge was spending more time with their cousin, Stacks. Stacks had just recently been released from prison. Her step-father was there with them, and had started his new truck driving job. As for Rika, motherhood was a bitch!

Rika had to wake up three hours early for school. Even though her mom watched Nila while Rika went to school, Queen still wanted Rika to feed Nila and get her dressed. Rodge was never at home these days. From time to time, he would tap on her window in the wee hours of the morning so Rika could let him in. One late night when he came, he had two big bags of diapers in his hands and a pocketful of money.

"Where did you get all this money from?" Rika asked with her eyes as big as a silver dollar.

"Don't worry about it, here go and buy you and your baby something. Tell her it's from her Uncle Rodge," he said, handing her a hundred-dollar bill.

Rika changed Nye's diaper, fed her, and they went back to sleep. The next morning, Rika still could not help wondering where Rodge was getting all that money. From that day on, she watched him like a hawk.

Chapter Seven

After a long night up with Nye, Rika still had to get up for school. That was her mother's way of showing her that being a mom came with a price. Her alarm clock went off at exactly 7 a.m. Still feeling groggy, she stumbled her way to the bathroom to get herself together. First, she looked in the living room to see if Rodge made it the night prior. To her surprise, there he was snuggled on the couch sound asleep. She tapped him a few times, before he acknowledged her presence.

"Rodge," Rika said in a whisper.

"What?" He asked, sounding like he had been working all night.

"Who let you in?"

"Mommy. Why?"

For a second, she thought she heard him wrong.

"Who?" Rika repeated.

"Mommy. I called her and let her know I was on my way home. I thought you needed your rest. What's up with all the questions?"

Rodge sure is acting strange these days. But, Rika didn't let her suspicion get the best of her. She just waited it out.

"Nothing, just wanted to know how you got in that's all."

She turned to walk away when he called her name.

"Rika, I gave Mama some money to take you shopping, so come straight home from school. Next week, it's a party in the projects. Don't trip. I already asked Mama if you can go. It's Five Deuce Day and the colors are red and black. If you need some school money, look in my pants pocket and get twenty dollars."

Rika had a thousand things going through her mind, like: *First of all, why aren't you getting ready for school? Second of all, since when did you become my damn daddy and start telling me when, where and how things are suppose to go?* Rika still didn't blow her cool. She simply nodded and got the twenty-dollar bill out of his pant pocket like she was told.

Rika's heart almost stopped when she saw the wad of hundreds before she even spotted a twenty. Her mind was racing a thousand miles a minute. She still couldn't think of how he was coming across all this kind of cash. One thing she did know was that the projects held a lot of unanswered questions, but she was getting to the bottom of this, one way or another.

Saturday night came and Rika couldn't wait. All of her sisters and cousins were going to the projects to celebrate whatever this "Five Deuce Day" that everybody was so hyped up about.

"I want Rika back here at a decent hour. Don't forget, she's only fourteen," Queen said, giving Rodge a dirty look.

"I got this covered baby!" Rodge shot back.

"Carima, you're the oldest. Make sure you watch out for her. Ain't nothing changed. And please don't bring her back pregnant."

"Trust me, I won't be coming back knocked up. I learned my lesson," Rika said as she bent down to give Nye a kiss on the forehead.

Little did Queen know, Rika had other things in mind -- like finding out how Rodge was coming up with all this cash. On that note, they all piled in Justine's 1989 Ford Escort (and, trust me, they were piled in). On the ride there, they were smoking weed and drinking Boones Farm mixed with Seagram's Gin. That really didn't bother her until Rika saw Rodge light up a joint and pass it to Carima.

"Somebody let down the windows so Rika won't get a contact. The last thing we want is for her to go home high," Shansi said.

Now, Shansi was one of her other cousins. She was a little close to her in age, and they kind of looked somewhat alike.

"Please roll 'em down. Mama would kill me if she came in fucked up. Hell, I had to give her a bill just to keep Nye and let her hang out," Rodge said, shaking his head as if he could picture the scene already.

Oh yeah! Rika thought to herself. What they didn't know was she had already been smoking. Once, when Nye had just come home from the hospital, they had to stay at her aunt's house because they were repainting the house. She was hanging out in Carima's room. They sometimes sneaked out through the back door of Rika's aunt's house late at night. Carima began to stir.

"Where you going?" Rika asked her.

"On the back porch. Wanna come?" She replied.

"What's out there?" Rika asked.

"Going to smoke a joint," Carima said.

Rika thought back to when Boogie warned her not to ever smoke. But hell, he was the father of her child and he wasn't doing shit. So, his words no longer had an effect on her. *What the hell?* Rika thought. That was one of the worst mistakes she had made in a long time. Her thoughts were interrupted when she heard everybody singing the lyrics to Dana Danes "Cindafella," and she immediately chimed in:

> *"I jumped in the Volvo and went on my way, I*
> *got to the party bout ten I say it was after*
> *eleven when I rocked the mic, and by the time*
> *I left the stage the people were hype. The*
> *princess was staring in disbelief\"*

And with that, the car was off and they had begun to get out. Rika didn't know where her head was because, by the time she stepped out of the car, people were everywhere. She had never seen anything like this in her life. Red and black was all you could see. Rodge sure didn't lie. Rika noticed Rodge giving different dudes dap, and girls were coming up to him hugging him like he was somebody well known.

Shansi was already talking to some guy rocking a jheri curl with rings on every finger. She motioned for Rika to come over to where she was so she could introduce Rika to him, at least that's what Rika thought. But it wasn't him, she was introducing Rika to the guy's relative.

"Rika, this is N-Sane. N-Sane, this is Rika."

"Hi," Rika said with a straight face.

"What's up baby?" He replied, as sexy as can be.

Before Rika walked away, she checked him out from head to toe. He was wearing a red and black Pendleton with black Dickeys and some red Chucks. They locked eyes before parting ways. She wasn't there to meet anybody. She was there on a mission. By the time Rika made it to where Carima and Justine were, Rodge was nowhere to be found. She looked around like she had heard somebody was shooting.

"What's wrong, Rika?" Carima asked.

"Where did Rodge disappear to?"

Rika was trying to calm down somewhat.

"Over there with Stack," Carima said pointing in their direction.

"Oh, okay," she said, making sure not to let him out of her sight.

While she was standing there, Rika couldn't help notice this small group of girls dressed in all red with black writing on the back of their jackets. It read, "52 Pueblo Bishop Blood Gang," and each one of them had their names in the top left corner on the front. It was obvious they were drunk because they were loud and singing songs that nobody heard but them. They all had bottles of Old English 800 in their hands except one of them. She had something call Super Socko.

Even though they seemed to be making fools of themselves, Rika was feeling their vibe. Then, she started to feel uncomfortable because she looked like she was fresh out of a Madonna video with the 1980 Material Girl tights and pumps on. She even started to go and sit in the car for the rest of the night, but that wasn't about to happen. She had work to do. *Speaking of which, where is Rodge?*

Just as Rika was about to turn and look, she looked into the eyes of a guy that looked scary as shit! For a few seconds, she thought her heart had stopped. She tried not to let him see her trying to swallow the lump in her throat. *Oh hell naw! This is some bullshit. She don't see how these people can stand out in the middle of the street with the music blaring, drinking, smoking, and only God knows what ever else.* Her heart really started pounding when she saw him approaching them.

"What's up, Carima? Is this Lil' Rika? She sure have grown up," he said, now smiling at her with the whitest teeth Rika had seen in a long time.

For some reason, this guy started to look familiar.

"Yeap, she have gotten big, uhh? Rika do you remember Detonate?"

Rika tried to play like she didn't, but she really did. He used to live across from Carima right here in the projects. She gave a simple smile. He must have got the hint real quick because, on that note, he took the first exit.

"You sure you don't remember him?" Carima asked with a curious tone.

"Hell yeah, I remember who he is. I didn't like him then and, from the way he look, I don't think I'll like him now," she said.

While they were still standing there, a guy rolled up in a wheelchair. He had a hat with a "P" on it, a red Dickies suit with some black gloves, and black house shoes on. Even though he was in a wheelchair, he was quite handsome, with eyes that would make your panties fall off just by looking into them. From the looks of things, he appeared to be very young. Rika wanted to ask him what happened to him, but she figured she'd wait and ask Carima on the way home.

There had to be something between them by the way Carima was talking and grinning from ear to ear. While they were talking, a lady walked up smelling like a barrel of fish. She was wearing pink pants and a lime green shirt. Her shoes were run down to the ground, and her eyes were as big as a fist.

"You got something," she asked, digging in her pocket and pulling out a few dollars and some change.

"Naw. Go over there and ask Rodge," the guy in the wheelchair said.

Ask Rodge for what? Rika thought. *What the hell do he have that she could possibly want?* She watched her as she made her way towards Rodge and Stacks. Whatever she said, he dug in his pocket and handed it to her, and she gave him the money then off she went. *I knew I was on to something! Now I know he is selling something, but I just don't know what.* Her eyes were glued to him, and he must have felt her starring because he looked dead at her and started smiling. He made his way to where they were standing. He had a stupid look on his face that read "GUILTY" all over it. *What was he thinking? I don't know what he was selling, but this sure was a good time to find out.*

"What's up, Rika? Why are you all in my business? Naw, I'm just playing. What's wrong with you?"

"Nothing. What did that lady want that you have? Who is she?" She was trying to hold back her tears.

"Look, you don't have nothing to worry about, it's just a few rocks," he said. "I can't stand to see Mama struggling to take care of us. I was the man of the house while Willie C was gone, and that made me feel good to slip money in her purse. I like giving you money to go to school and buy your baby nice things. You feel me? So, don't trip. Everything will be okay."

"Do Mama know?"

"I think she's suspicious, but she haven't just flat out asked me like you just did."

"So, that explains everything -- the clothes, diapers, and all the money you've been just freely handing over. Does this mean you're a baller now?"

"Hell naw, and I'm far from becoming one too. And what do you know about a baller?" He responded, laughing.

"I'm not stupid you know," Rika said, letting him know that she knew more about the streets than he gave her credit for.

"Are you having fun?" Rodge asked.

"Well, if you call standing in the middle of the street drinking and listening to music fun, then I guess. How do you know all these people?"

"You know 'em too, you just probably don't remember them. Loosen up and just have fun, you know. Just be glad that you're out of the house for a while," he said, winking at Rika.

"Since you said it like that, then I guess I will. Hey, where's everybody at?" She said looking around.

"Having fun," he exclaimed, and they both laughed.

Chapter Eight

It was six o'clock in the morning when Precious's alarm clock went off. She knew she couldn't waste any time getting the kids up and ready for school. She rolled out of bed and headed straight to the bathroom to brush her teeth and wash her face. Once she had gotten herself together, she headed to the kitchen to start breakfast. One thing about Precious, she was a country girl and she believed in taking care of her family.

Once in the kitchen, she prepared grits, bacon and her famous eggs with chopped red and green peppers and a few sprinkles of cheese. Then, it was time to wake the kids up so they could get ready for school. Precious went downstairs in the basement to wake the boys up one by one. Since there was only one bathroom, she didn't feel like hearing all the bickering.

She decided to wake up Calvin first. He was the oldest of her boys and very simple, he didn't have to do much. As long as he had on clean clothes and food in his stomach, he was fine. After waking him up and getting him out of the bathroom quickly, she then went to wake up Eddie. Eddie was a little different from Calvin. He needed some extra coaching. He had to be dragged out of bed some mornings, and Precious was glad to know that this wasn't one of those mornings. After they were up and ready, she decided it was time to wake up Showboat. But, to her surprise, he was wide awake.

"What you doing up so early?" Precious asked with a shaky voice because her had startled her.

"I heard you when you was upstairs in the kitchen. I knew you were making breakfast," he said, taking the covers off and heading to the bathroom to get ready for school.

The truth of the matter was, Showboat learned to sleep light when he stayed with Pat because he never knew when something was going to jump off. For some reason, he felt a burst of excitement. He knew something good was going to come out of this day, but he didn't know what. He remembered talking to Kameisha on the phone for hours last night, and couldn't wait to see her, and get in her skins.

After getting the run around trying to enroll him in school, they finally made a decision. Showboat had two options: either go to Northwest High and be in the 10th Grade or go to Wilbur Middle School and be in the 9th Grade. He chose to go to Wilbur because he had spotted a thick little yellow bone by the name of Tonya. She was a proctor that gave new students a tour of the school. *Damn, she fine,* he said to himself. He had to think of something to make her laugh.

So, he said, "Damn, baby, you don't have to walk so fast."

He started trying to slow down his pace.

"Well, you need to hurry up then," she replied, with much attitude.

"Well, my legs don't move that fast," he said, with no good intentions.

She finally laughed.

"Can I have your number?"

"I kinda got a boyfriend"

"Well let me ask him," Showboat said, knowing that he could fight real well so that wouldn't be a problem.

"You bold I see."

"My momma told me you have to ask for what you want," he said.

When she laughed again, he knew he was all in. Once Showboat made it home from a long day, he raced to the phone to call Kameisha. After making plans to go to her house, he hung up the phone. Then, he went upstairs to talk it over with his dad, who had just made it home from work.

"What's up, Pops?" He asked, feeling extra cool.

"Nothing, son. Just tired as hell. Listen, take the keys and run to the store and get me a soda pop and some bread," he said sitting down at the table looking over the mail.

That was right up Showboat's alley. Now, he had a way over to Kameisha's house. He got the money from his dad, grabbed the keys from the key holder, and out the door he went. Showboat was cruising down 13th Street until he came to Grove and made a right. He took that straight down to 21st and made another right, then he made it to Spruce where Kameisha lived. He jumped out the car feeling it and knocked on the door.

Kameisha came to the door looking like the Black China doll that he remembered. She gave him one of those I-miss-you hugs, and they went inside. Showboat didn't stay long because he knew he was on borrowed time, so he got a quick kiss and headed for the door. In one swift motion, he jumped back into his ride and headed to the QuikTrip at 13th & Oliver.

Once inside, he noticed a little dude from down the way. He didn't think too much of it. He strolled in the store, got what Flint wanted, then he proceeded to the front door when he was blocked by the White boy from down the street. Showboat had seen this cat a couple of times, but he really didn't think to pay him any attention. He walked right past him. That's when it all began.

The White boy said, "Look at this nigger."

Showboat turned around and said, "What? Who you calling nigga?"

"I'm talking to you," the White boy replied,

Showboat said, "Naw. You can't be talking to me like that. You must be trying to get your head split open."

That's when his boys decided to jumped in, spewing out racial comments. Showboat shook his head, smiled his signature smile, and said, "It's okay. I got you," with a sly grin on his face.

Angry was an understatement. He was as hot as fish grease. He thought to himself, *If I ever see him again it's on and popping.* He made it to his father's house, handed his dad the keys, went downstairs and picked up his pocketknife, and headed out the door. He had only one thing in mind. He was going get this fool.

Showboat was walking down the street thinking to himself, *How could this dude be so disrespectful?* He walked up 13th and down to Hillside trying to calm himself down. Just when he came to his senses and realized it wasn't that serious, he headed back home. On his way up 17th Street, right before he got to Oliver, he noticed a blue van creeping up behind him. In it were the White boys from QuikTrip.

"What's up now, nigger? You think you are some bad ass? I will kill you."

Without hesitation, Showboat's street instincts kicked right in. As Showboat began to look around, he noticed a man working on a house, so he didn't want to make too many quick moves so he played it cool.

"Man, why are you following me? I haven't done anything to you."

The White boy replied, "Fuck you, nigger!"

Showboat made sure he kept his cool. So, he asked again, *"Why are you bothering me? I haven't done anything to you."*

But at the same time, he was giving the guy his signature smile. And, anybody who knew him knew that wasn't a good thing. It was actually dangerous. The van stopped and Showboat stayed calm.

Just when the White boy got out of the van and walked up to Showboat, he swung a 2x4 and tried to hit Showboat. In a flash, Showboat leaned back, then came forward and stuck him right in the stomach -- exposing all his intestines. The White boy looked at him in disbelief, as he grabbed the knife and fell to his knees. The rest of his friends looked on in horror! Little did Showboat know, the boy's mother was in the car.

She jumped out screaming, "You killed my son, you nigger."

Showboat looked down on the ground and watched the dude take his last breath and release his bowels. With a flash of light, Showboat took off running. He headed straight home. Before long, police cars, ambulance and fire trucks were everywhere. Of course, there were some people who saw the whole thing and they pointed the police in the direction Showboat ran. With nowhere to run, he ran into a neighbor's backyard and hid in a vacant doghouse.

When he thought the coast was clear, he ran straight home. When he ran in the house, he ran straight to the basement. Flint and Precious looked at each other with puzzled looks on their faces because he was sweating profusely. Before he could make it to the basement, she heard banging at her front door.

Precious came to the door and swung it open with much attitude and said, "May I help you?"

"Excuse me, ma'am. We're looking for gentlemen with a white T-shirt on," one of the officers said.

Precious replied, "I don't know what you're talking about. It ain't no boy in here with no white T-shirt on, and I don't know what you're talking about."

"Ma'am, can we search your house?" The other policeman asked.

"You sure cannot. Do you have a search warrant?" Precious responded.

"No, but I can get one," the first cop said.

Showboat was downstairs in the basement hiding when he heard the police officer say that he can get one. He did not know the place was surrounded by cops. He tried to crawl out of the basement window, and was met with a 9mm barrel right in his face.

"We got 'em," an officer yelled.

"Man, what's going on? Why are you all around here harassing me?" Showboat asked.

"You're coming downtown with us. We have a few questions for you."

"What kind of questions?"

"You'll see when we get down there."

When they brought Showboat from the backyard of his house, news cameras from every news station in Wichita were there. On the way down to the police station, all Showboat could think about was, *It was either him or me, and I wasn't go out like that. I wasn't bothering anybody. They brought it to me, so I had to do what I had to do.*

But, deep down inside, Showboat knew there was a better way. Yet, at this point, exactly what that was eluded him. With no time for thinking about what could've happened, he knew he had to figure out what he must do to get himself out of this dire dilemma.

Chapter Nine

Five years had passed since Rika had moved back to Los Angeles, and a lot had changed since then. Little Nila had grown up to be such a beautiful little girl. She was chocolate with beautiful long hair, and eyes that will light up the sky. Her smile was as beautiful as any Caribbean sunset. She was Rika's everything. No matter what kind of day she was having, all Nila had to do was flash one of those sunset smiles, and everything that was bothering her would fade away.

A young mother, Rika didn't know where she would be without her Nye. All the bad things people had to say, all the things that she had been through, were nothing compared to the love they shared. Although she ran away from home, she still had access to see Nila anytime she wanted. That was something that her mother always allowed. During this time that Rika moved away from home, so much happened. She started using drugs and hanging out with four of her best friends (Bomb, Wanda, Peaches, and Faith).

Bomb got her name because she backed down from nothing. Whether it was male or female, whatever it took to take them down, she was going to get the job done. The only thing about Bomb, she had a dark side to her. Nobody really knew where she came from. She just came out of the blue, and she became one of their closest friends. She stood about 5'6" and weighed about 165 pounds but was very light on her feet. She had long, kinky hair and smooth pecan skin with bowlegs.

When it came to fighting, she had mastered the art. She was known to give men a good run for their money, and women didn't even stand a chance. That's where her name came from. "Bomb," because she was always going take the first punch, period. But there was something about her eyes. They were cold and dark. Rika never really understood why they befriended her, because it was something about her that just didn't sit well with none of them. It wasn't a fear though, but it was something.

Wanda, on the other hand, was more laid-back. She was the thickest of them all. Some called her fat, but she thought she was beautiful. She was 5'4" and weighed about 195 pounds. The girl could dress her face off! And, make-up was not even an art for her, it was something she could do with her eyes closed. Although she was beautiful, Wanda didn't understand her true worth, and often times she would let others take advantage of her. She was a hustler by nature, and that was passed down from her mom and uncles.

Now, Peaches was just flat out crazy. She came from a background of singers, and the girl could sing like a canary. Because she came from a gospel background, whenever she was feeling down and out, Rika would have Peaches sing her favorite church song, "Precious Lord." Peaches was a lot like Rika. They both were raised on the pew and they were no strangers to who God was. They would often laugh at times and say they were the prodigal daughters. And, because they had those things in common, they had a tighter bond than the others.

They understood things more spiritual. Sometimes, they would get drunk and sit down and have some very deep conversations. They both knew they were not where they were supposed to be. They were not living up to the calling that was placed on their lives.

But Faith, she was just that, Faith! She didn't come around that often, but it seemed like she came around just when Rika needed her. Faith had a job even though she was 16 years old with a little boy. Brandon was her world. He gave her life.

Faith was their voice of reason. Whenever they got into trouble, it would be Faith that came to talk sense into them. She was like that angel on your right shoulder telling you, "Everything is going to be alright," and, "This too shall pass." And, when Faith would hug you, it was almost like you were hugging God himself. Sometimes, she would just hold Rika in her arms and rock her until she would calm down.

Make no mistake about it, she was by no means game goofy. She was straight out of the hood. In fact, she was a member of one of the roughest project gangs in L.A. After she was held at gunpoint and shot at close range with a sawed off shotgun and lost one of her lungs, she decided to hang up her flag. Shortly after she retired, she lost he brother, the father of her child, and her two aunts. That did it. She realized it wasn't worth it.

She had a son to raise and nobody could raise him better than her. Faith went back to school and earned her GED. She was now working at Louisiana's Chicken on Manchester and Figueroa, and was renting a room in her cousins' house. She would drop her son off with his grandparents while she was working. Life was going well for her for the most part, but she too was battling her own demons. The difference between Faith and the rest of them was she knew where her help came from, and she utilized it every chance she got.

"Rika, wake up!"

When Rika opened her eyes, Bomb was standing over her pointing a 9mm in her face.

"Why do you always do that? I've told you more than once, I don't like that shit," Rika said.

Bomb would sometimes just watch Rika sleep for hours, and the shit was rather creepy. They would almost come to blows about it, and all Bomb would say was, "If I wanted to kill you, it would be easy. You should be glad all I'm doing is watching you sleep."

Her words were cold and dry. Rika knew something wasn't right with this picture, but the truth was, she was especially afraid of her after witnessing her kill a few people that crossed her or didn't pay her when they were supposed to.

"Shut the fuck up and get dressed. You always got something to say. You're not going to be satisfied until I do something bad to you," Bomb said.

Bomb always made threats about hurting somebody, and she was known for doing just that. For some reason, when it came to Rika, it seemed that Bomb had some kind of hate in her heart for Rika. Rika knew in her heart that it was just a matter of time before Bomb acted on it. But, for now, Rika would just lay low and let this thing play out.

While they were cruising down 83rd and McKinley heading over to Wanda's house to pick her up so they can go to the Fox Hills Mall, they were talking about how the Bishops were throwing a party that night. Everybody that was somebody was gonna be there, so they had to be dressed for the occasion. Once they arrived at Wanda's house, they noticed the door was cracked. Bomb had no problem just walking straight in. The TV was blaring loud and clothes were everywhere. It looked like someone had been fighting or was in some sort of struggle. Bomb took her 9mm out of the small of her back.

As they headed toward the bedroom door that was closed, Bomb had motioned for Rika to be quiet as they eased up on the door. Just when they were about to kick the door in, they heard Wanda talking to a man who sounded like Jelly, one of Bomb's old flings. With the strangest look on her face, Bomb shook her head and kicked in the door. And, what do we see?

"What the hell," Bomb yelled.

In that instance, she began to go crazy. Wanda and Jelly both were startled. Bomb had found them with no clothes on and the smell of sex in the air. Bomb went into a full rage, screaming and waving her gun around.

"I'm about to kill this bitch!"

Bomb jumped on top of the bed and began to pistol whip Wanda. All you saw was blood and teeth everywhere. Jelly knew to get somewhere. He scooped up his clothes and headed toward the door. But, that did not save Wanda from Bomb's wrath.

"Stop! Stop it! You're going to kill her," Rika yelled out.

"Bitch, I knew you was grimy," Bomb said to Wanda as she continued to pounce on her.

Rika grabbed Bomb by her legs and dragged her off of Wanda. Rika knew Wanda was dead. She just knew it. Bomb was still swinging wildly and screaming stuff that she could not even understand. All Rika was trying to do was get her out of there. Rika felt bad for Wanda, but she knew she was wrong and she did have a bad habit of sleeping with other people's men. That was not the first time, and neither will it be the last time somebody beat her ass about it if she survived that.

Once they got to the car, Rika started screaming, "What the fuck is wrong with you? You act like some crazed lunatic!"

Bomb was paying Rika no attention. She was driving reckless down Manchester. By the time they got to Florence and made that right, all reason and logic went out the window. They thought they spotted Jelly's car and the Chase was on. By the time they made it to Florence and Central, they had run three red lights, almost hit two pedestrians, and ran over a couple of curbs. Bomb realized it wasn't Jelly's car at all. It just so happened to be a young Hispanic mother with her children in the backseat.

"Let me out this mutherfucka! I'll catch the bus. You're crazy and out-of-control! I can't believe you just did that. I can't believe that you're so angry and upset when you do the same type of dirt, just in a different way. Can you call the kettle black? If they really knew who you really were, I promise you, the tables would turn quick."

As soon as those words left her mouth, Rika regretted them. Bomb gave Rika the coldest, deadliest look she had ever seen in her life. The words that came out of her mouth next let Rika know that Bomb had some serious issues, not just with the people around her but within herself.

"You know what, I'mma let you slide. I don't know what kind of grace and mercy you got on your life today, but just know this: Today is your lucky day, you aught to be glad that something in me won't let me hurt you."

Her words sent chills through Rika, and it seemed like they echoed in her brain for months, weeks and days on. Bomb decided to let her out at the nearest bus stop. Rika really didn't want to go home because, at this point, she didn't trust Bomb. Rika just want her out of her life for good. She'd had enough. She had seen enough. She was over her. The only thing that she was thinking about was making her way back to Wanda's house to make sure she was okay, but Rika was afraid because she didn't know if she was dead or not or if Bomb was going back. Because Wanda was her girl, those were chances she was willing to take. So, she headed straight back to check on Wanda.

Chapter Ten

After days of interrogation, Showboat was exhausted. When he was finally able to make his first phone call, he made it to his step-mom, Precious.

"You have a collect call from Bentley (that was Showboat's biological name) from the Sedgwick County Jail. To accept this call, Press '1.' If you do not accept, simply hang up," the recording directed. "Beep!"

Precious immediately pressed 1.

"Hello."

"Hi, son. How are you hanging in there?"

"As well as can be expected. I'm exhausted and frustrated. I haven't had any sleep, and they keep coming in here asking me the same questions that I answered two days ago. Every time I ask them what are my charges they don't answer."

Precious was livid. What Bentley didn't know was that she had already contacted the NAACP and they were all over it. Not to mention, the victim's mother was on every news channel referring to him as "that nigger!" For the last two days, Precious and everyone in their family were glued to the news when they announced he would be charged with criminal homicide. Apparently, Bentley hadn't heard the news.

"Baby, everything will work out. Just have faith."

Bentley wanted to say so much, but he felt so defeated. So he decided to do what he always did when he was faced with opposition, just shut down. Precious knew him very well, so she knew exactly what he was doing. So, at this point, she decided to let him know that the NAACP had decided to get involved. Bentley was so ecstatic to hear the news, he almost couldn't control his excitement.

But, on the other hand, he didn't know what the outcome would really be. That night, Bentley laid on his cot thinking about what his life will be after this. Shortly after hanging up from Precious, Bentley heard his name being called.

"Bentley, roll to go."

That was music to his ears. He jumped up and grabbed what little he came in with and headed toward the door. After signing all of his paperwork and returning the greasy orange jumpsuit, he was free to go. Once he exited the last elevator, he was greeted by his girlfriend Tonya along with Precious and Flint.

Flint had a real serious look on his face. Precious seemed relieved. And, Tonya was just happy to see her man back on the street. His dad didn't know what was going on, but he sure wasn't about to rollover and let them railroad his son.

"Get in the car, and let's roll."

They had business to discuss. One thing he was not playing about was his son's freedom. Showboat gave Tonya a quick kiss and assured her he will call her later. With that, he turned and left. The next morning, Flint woke him up bright and early.

"Wake up dude."

Without hesitation, Bentley jumped out of bed and headed straight to the shower. Flint Didn't speak another word. They jumped in his car and headed straight to the attorney. After filling out what seemed like books of paperwork, they were finally able to see Will Stewart.

After an hour into their free consultation, Will explained to them what they were up against and what his fees were. To even go before the judge, he wanted $10,000 -- not to mention if it went to trial, that was another $30,000. That wasn't too much for Flint to handle. The problem he had was Attorney Stewart couldn't guarantee anything. When the lawyer saw he wasn't dealing with just any old type of cat, he decided to speak the truth.

"The prosecuting attorney, Susan Dickson, is in her first year as the District Attorney, and this would be her first major case. And, as far as Will knew, she might not want to take the case if she wasn't 500% sure she could beat it."

With all of the attention the mother was getting, and not to mention her trying to get Bentley murdered, Will felt it could be risky but he couldn't be too sure. Will's recommendation to Bentley was to lay low until he found out the outcome. Once they made it home, Flint got in touch with one of his nieces who had married a guy in the Navy and who was now stationed in Guam. She agreed to let Bentley come over there with her.

Flint wasn't playing any games about his son and he never did. He was his oldest and his junior. And, as a father, Flint had to do whatever to protect him. Bentley knew it too. He saw his father rise up yet again on his behalf and that made all the difference in the world to him.

The idea of him moving to Guam was very short lived when they received the phone call a few days later that the DA had dropped all charges. Everybody came to congratulate him. Some of his older uncles came just to give him those long lectures that seemed to last forever, but he knew not to wear it on his face because that would have been trouble.

Since the murder had taken place, Bentley was trying to lay low, but that still didn't stop how he truly felt about it. He had some resentment pertaining to his actions. He still wrestled with the fact that he had to be put in a predicament like that and since then it seemed like his life went from sugar to shit overnight.

The only time he felt a sense of relief was when he performed with his band, the Ru Boys.

They were like a brotherhood. They enjoyed what they did. Not to mention, the ladies were swarming from everywhere.

Although he felt some sense of release, this still hadn't stopped the agonizing pain that he felt about the way his life has shifting. Not only was he dealing with the things that were going on at home, but Showboat was also dealing with the fact that every time the Ru Boys would get into any type of trouble, it was him that would always seem to land in jail. No matter how many people were out there fighting, no matter who started the fight, he became a police magnet and in his mind it just wasn't fair. *Why was this always happening to me?* He was tired of it. He was sick of it. He knew something had to change.

Although Bentley and Kameisha were on again off again, and she just so happened to have his first baby. There was something about Tonya that he really loved. Theirs was a love like no other, because he knew she truly loved him. When everything seemed to fall apart, she knew how to make things seem just right. But, even with her, he knew it wasn't all that it seemed.

She claimed to have a baby by him as well, however, the baby looked just like her and had none of his features. There were times when he would take different family members to her house to see the baby, and they would take one look and shake their head and make little wisecracks like, "He's a handsome little thing."

But once they were outside, they would let him know, "Man, that's not your baby. That baby is a redbone."

This would make him feel so bad. He wished it really was his child. Deep down inside, he knew it wasn't his baby, but he just wanted it to be real bad.

One night, Bentley got real drunk while he was hanging out with a couple of his cousins. He just couldn't believe all the chain of events that had taken place in his life. It seemed like they were all rushing up on him at the same time. He knew he couldn't start crying, because he would look like a coward. So, he did what he had always done, and that's bottle it up inside.

For the first time in his life, he wanted something different. Something more solid, not so chaotic, and not so emotionally draining. He wasn't a very spiritual person, nor was he a believer of anything higher than himself. But one thing that he did know if there were a "God," "He" needed to change the situation immediately.

Chapter Eleven

By the time Rika made it to Wanda's block, police and ambulance were everywhere. She didn't know whether to walk up to the house or to run. That was, until she spotted Peaches coming out of the house wearing an expression that she could not read.

"Fuck it," Rika said out loud, "I'm here now."

Once she got closer to the house, she noticed the police and everybody else were just posted up, chilling. *Did she die?* Rika wondered. Her thought was quickly interrupted when Peaches spotted Rika and began to call out her name. Rika didn't know if she should run or what. Just as the thought came, it left when Peaches gave her a warm smile and headed in her direction. Upon contact, they embraced each other and Peaches broke the silence.

"She's going to be okay, Rika. They're going to take her in to get a few stitches, and then she should be released. You know these clowns nowadays is a trip."

Getting right in her ear she whispered, "You know, Jelly is responsible for this. He tried to rob her, and once he couldn't get any money or drugs, he rapped and beat her up pretty bad."

Rika could not believe her ears. In a state of confusion, and just flat out disbelief, she tried to make some sense out of what she had just heard. Rape? Robbery gone bad? What the hell? Why was she lying? She knew damn well who was responsible for this, or maybe this was Peaches trying to lure her over to the cops so she could be arrested. Whatever it was, Rika was totally confused and she wanted to see for herself what was really going on.

So, she headed straight toward the house. Right before Rika got to the front door, they were bringing her out on a stretcher. She looked to see what type of damage Bomb caused and, to her surprise, she had a few cuts, a few knots and some bruises. When she saw her and smiled, there were no teeth missing. Now, she knew something strange was going on. She was right there. She could've sworn she saw teeth flying and blood splattering. Rika thought she was going crazy for a moment, but she shook it off and returned the smile.

"Everything is gonna be okay. Right?" Rika asked.

It sounded like a statement, but was more of a question in Rika's own eyes. Wanda nodded and they wheeled her off into the ambulance. Peaches and she stood on the porch, and she began to give her the version that Wanda gave her. Rika wanted to tell her what really happened, but she really didn't know what to say so she played it cool and kept it to herself. She was going to get to the bottom of this once and for all. She knew her eyes could not be deceiving her. Rika know just what she saw because she was there.

Peaches and Rika decided to stick to their original plan. They went to the mall, got their clothes for the party, laughed like old times, and made plans for the night ahead. Being with Peaches was like a breath of fresh air. There were no strings attached. They could talk about a lot of stuff, there was nothing that they couldn't really talk about. They would reminisce about old times -- how they used to pray together during times that they didn't seem to think everything would be okay, but things would turn out just fine.

She was peaceful. Rika didn't feel like she had to watch her back. She looked out for Rika and she went out for her. They decided to go to Peaches house to get dressed and drink their favorite drink (gin and super juice). Peaches put on DJ Quake's "Tonight Is The Night" and they got their groove on as they got dressed.

That night was amazing! They had so much fun. She hated to think of it like this, but she totally was glad that Wanda and Bomb were not with them. It just seemed like, whenever they were around, it was so stressful and heavy. They always had to watch what they did and what they said.

Whenever they were around, it was just trouble. If it wasn't Bomb trying to fight somebody thinking they were looking at her funny, it was Wanda screwing somebody's man in the bathroom and then getting into it with some other woman about her man. But with Peaches it was just all fun. After the party was over, as they were walking to their car, they ran into an old friend they used to hang out with years ago named Taz. Back in the day, Taz had a few run-ins with Bomb because they were both two strong women. And, just like Bomb wouldn't back down, neither would Taz.

Taz was different from Bomb. She knew who she was and she didn't have to prove anything. She didn't go out of her way to make herself look good. She was just that type of a person, and Rika thought Bomb was threatened by Taz. She was gorgeous. She had her own money. And, she just didn't put up with the bull crap. For the most part, she was downright legit.

"What's going on with y'all? What are you about to get into?' Taz asked while extending her warm hand and, thus, the blunt.

"Nothing. Pretty much 'bout to go to the house in Chino for a minute. Why? What you got going on?" Rika asked, taking the blunt from her hand and inhaling it.

"Shit, nothing. About to role the streets for minute. You know how I do it. Wanna roll?"

Rika looked at Peaches, Peaches looked at Rika, and they said let's do it. They jumped in her decked-out 98 and headed towards Compton. That was her stomping grounds. They pulled up, first, in front of Skateland to see what was popping off. It wasn't too much of nothing, so they decided to see what the Pirus were up to. They pulled up on 137th & Avalon, and cars were everywhere. It seemed like they were having a party of their own. And, since they were already dressed for the occasion, they decided to jump out and enjoy the festivities.

"Damn, everybody is here," Peaches announced.

"Hell yeah. I think I see a few baby daddies in the house," Taz chimed in.

They all fell out laughing. Taz went under her seat, grabbed some kush, and rolled another blunt. They sat in the car for a few minutes inhaling the herbal refreshments before they exited the car. When they were about to walk in, it seemed like the party was ending because everybody started heading out of the front door.

"Damn. Did we miss it?" Rika asked in disbelief, more like disappointment because she was high, feeling good, and was ready to party even harder now.

Big J-Rock was coming out of the door right when Rika said that and was like, "No, little mama.

We all about to head toward the beach now. Y'all wanna roll?"

"I'm in the passenger seat, so it's up to them if they want to go or not." Rika said.

The truth of the matter is, they all knew what jumped off at the beach. It was just a hook-up ground for the on-night stands, and Rika really wasn't into all that. So, she looked over at her crew to see where their heads were. They all collectively agreed.

"Naw."

"We cool."

"We'll pass this time."

"What," Big J-Rock said. "Y'all scared or something? We don't bite."

"No, it's not that at all. We just was ready to party, so since the party's over, we might as well head to the house so we could chill or something. We'll catch up with you later."

With that, they headed off the porch and toward the car. Being that they parked far, they were passing all kind of cars -- Cadillacs on Dayton's, Glass Houses (Impalas) dressed up. All the rats were out dressed in dental floss, leaving nothing to the imagination, and jumping in different cars with different dudes.

Well, that wasn't too foreign. Rika was known to do that herself from time to time. Tonight just wasn't one of those nights for her though. Rika was feeling good, looking good, and she just didn't want some stranger all over her. She just wasn't in the mood for that tonight. Plus, Rika didn't see nothing there that was worth it.

Right before they reached Taz's car, Peaches spotted one or her regular late-night creeps, Junebug. June had long paper and didn't mind spending. Back in the day, he used to be a nobody. Now that he has money, all the chickenheads be in his face. He and Peaches have a long history that goes way back to when they were 14 years old. This was the first boy that Peaches ever had sex with.

They had a genuine love for each other, but, for some reason when he grew up and realized that he wasn't as bad looking as he thought, women came from everywhere and he began to lose sight of the one woman that was down with him when he didn't have nothing but a broke down Pinto and some beat up Crocker Sacks (with the flaps and taps). That really hurt Peaches because she thought they had would last forever. Now, don't get it wrong, if she ever needed or wanted anything, he was right there.

When her mom passed away, he paid for the funeral and everything. She didn't want for anything and she never has when it came to June. The only thing that he didn't provide was his undivided attention. He knew where his bread was buttered though. He knew he could trust her. So anytime he got into any trouble or anything else for that matter, it was Peaches that he called.

When he needed to stash his dope, he stashed it at her house. In fact, he's the reason she has a house. They were the type of people that were supposed to be together but weren't due to whatever reason. Everyone he messed with knew about her, and that tended to cause problems for her sometimes. Anywhere from fights to phone calls to slashed tires. You name it, women have done it to her. And, every time they would bust her windows out or spray paint her car, Junebug was right there to replace it and add to whatever it was that they damaged.

"Sup, baby? What you about to get into?" June asked.

"Nothing. About to go home and chill. How about you?"

"About to go to the beach now. Y'all rolling?"

"Naw, we gone let y'all have this one."

"C'mon. I got y'all."

Peaches looked at Rika.

Rika said, "It's whatever."

They turned to see what Taz was going to do, and she was all up in some clown's face.

"Taz, what you gone do? June want us the roll to the beach with him. You going, or are you staying?" Peaches asked.

"I'mma chill, y'all go and have fun. I'll catch up with y'all later. Rika, you still got my phone number right?" Todd asked.

"Yeah. I'll hit you up tomorrow or something."

"Okay, bet."

On that note, they jumped in the car with June and headed toward the beach. That night was so fun and so relaxing, Rika did not want it to end. By the time they pulled up to Peaches' car, the sun was up. Rika stumbled out of the backseat, said her goodbyes, and went and sat in the car. When they made it to Peaches' house, they were exhausted. They showered, smoked another blunt, and went to sleep. By the time they woke up, it was about 6:00 p.m. Still drained, Peaches cooked dinner and they sat on the couch and reflected on the past events. She asked whether Rika heard from Bomb.

Rika told her, "Not in a few days."

Peaches had this weird look on her face. She asked, "Do you really trust her?"

It caught Rika off guard because she thought Peaches really liked Bomb.

"Why do you ask me that?" Rika asked.

"I wouldn't say all that. We're cordial. It's something about her that don't sit too well with me. I don't think she is who she say she is."

She was confused, so Rika asked Peaches, "What you mean by that?"

"I don't know. Just keep your eyes open. Maybe it's just me, but I just get this strange feeling every time she's around."

The truth of the matter was, Rika totally understood that because she felt the same way. It was almost like Bomb had a hidden agenda. It was something about her that just didn't sit well with Rika either, but she kept it to herself. She knew she would get to the bottom of it one way or another.

There was an awkward silence as they both stared into space. She didn't know what Peaches was thinking about, but Rika was thinking about how Bomb had attacked Wanda and how the story changed within hours. For now, Rika wouldn't say too much of nothing, but she must go pay Wanda a visit soon.

Chapter Twelve

For the next couple of days, Rika camped out at Peaches house. They laughed, talked and just simply enjoyed each other's company. It was always a pleasure spending time with her. She was like a little sister that Rika never had, and she knew how to bring out the best in Rika and help her see things from a different perspective. At this point in her life, Rika really needed that. Although she was fighting her own demons, she thought she hid it pretty well.

When she was only 16 years old, Rika ran away from home. By the time she was 17, she was homeless and on crack cocaine. She knew if she didn't change her ways soon that she would become a product of the streets. Rika really didn't understand how her life had turned out the way that it did. She would often ask herself, *Where did I go wrong? How did my life get to this point?* She knew she was better than that. She knew this couldn't be the end for her.

There were times the only place Rika had to sleep was in a vacant house, or on a park bench. Rika even remembers the time when she was hanging out in the projects (Pueblo del Rio) late at night and she was tired of wondering around looking for somebody's couch to camp out on.

Someone left their comforter hanging on the clothesline to dry, so she looked around, snatched it off the line, and went into a vacant apartment to crash for the night. Rika woke up to all kinds of voices right in the next room. There were all kinds of people smoking crack and shooting up heroin.

Rika thought to herself, *Wow! They could've came in here and killed me or, even worse, raped me.* Rika shook her head in mere disgust. She jumped up wiped her face and eased out of the back door. Once she got outside, she began to cry, *Why is this happening to me? What did I do so bad to deserve this?* With nowhere to turn, Rika went to Rodge's house. Rodge and Meeka had been dating for a while now, and since it was morning, she knew they were awake. When she knocked on the door, Meeka answered.

"Hey, girl. Where you coming from?"

"Around. Where's my brother?"

"He's in there with the baby," Meeka answered, looking at Rika suspect. "Are you hungry?"

"Yeah, did you cook breakfast?" Rika asked, heading straight for the kitchen.

"Girl, you better wash your hands before you go in my pots."

Rika laughed and went in the bathroom to wash her hands. One thing about Meeka, she could cook. And, even though she was from L.A., she cooked like she was from the country. By the time

Rika came out of the bathroom, Meeka had made her plate and was pouring her some orange juice. Meeka and Rika were real good friends before she and her brother even started dating. Rika was always welcomed at her house. She made sure Rika was straight. So, she had her own relationship with Meeka.

She was someone Rika could sit back and laugh and talk with, and even cry with. This was rare for Rika. There were even times they cried together. She loved her like Rika was her blood sister, and it was a special bond they couldn't quite explain. But one thing that Rika knew was that Meeka loved her unconditionally. Rika sat there for a minute trying to figure out her next move.

The truth of the matter is, when you're homeless, hungry, down and out, nobody really wants to deal with you unless they love you for real. Rika learned that early in the game. And, even though she could always go back home, she was too stubborn and hardheaded. She didn't want to follow her mother's rules. Her mother was old-school.

Her attitude was, "If you want to be grown, I'll treat you like your grown."

With that statement, she made a true believer out of her and left her ass right in them streets. Rika knew that had to be hard for her mother though, knowing that her baby girl was roaming the streets of Los Angeles with no supervision -- treading very dangerous ground and encountering life or death situations. She knew she had to really trust God to be able to sleep at night.

She would often tell her siblings, "I don't care what she do. Y'all better not never see her hungry or going without because she's still y'all sister."

And they did just that. That's why it was okay for her to pop up at Rodge's house. Or, if she saw her sister, Justine, in the streets, Justine bought Rika clothes, shoes and whatever else she thought she needed. Her sister, Camille, would come find her sometimes in the projects and make Rika go stay with her. But, there was something about Rika wanting to do things her own way that kept her in a lot of trouble. She thought she was grown. She thought she was doing something. But, at the end of the day, Rika was only hurting herself and the people around her who truly loved her.

The one person that Rika was hurting the most was her daughter. Rika's baby loved her no matter what state of mind Rika was in. There were times that her mother would bring her to see Rika and she would be drunk as hell, talking all kinds of crazy. Rika even remembered, one time, Queen brought Nila to Carima's house to spend some time with Rika, and Rika was coming down off one of her binges. She threw up everywhere, and there Nila was trying to clean it up.

When Rika came to, she just wanted to fall off the face of the earth. *What was I good for? What was my purpose here on earth?* She had so many questions going through her mind. Nila didn't care. All she cared about was being with Rika. That hurt, and it seemed like it cut so deep.

Not only did it hurt, but she was embarrassed. Rika was ashamed to call herself a mother. That led Rika into deeper darkness. She tried not to let Meeka see her tear up, so Rika hurried up and scarfed her food down and left the house before Rodge came out of the room.

She decided to go pay Faith a visit at her job. Once Rika arrived at McDonald's, Faith was working in the drive-thru. When Faith saw Rika walk into the building, she gave her a big smile and mouthed, "I'll be off in about an hour." So, Rika sat down and made herself comfortable.

As she sat there, staring out of the window, her mind would not rest. It felt like it was moving so fast that if it didn't calm down soon, it would explode any second. *All of these thoughts. Too many to even put into any type of order!* So, Rika decided to close her eyes and take a deep breath.

"What the fuck?" She said it out loud before she could even catch herself.

Rika looked around to make sure she didn't draw any unnecessary attention to herself. Thank goodness she didn't. The only person's attention she had caught was Faith. Once Faith had clocked out, she came to where Rika was sitting and shook her keys in Rika's face.

"I got a car," Faith said with a wide grin.

"That what's up! What kind did you get?" Rika asked.

"A 1990 Toyota Camry. Let's take a spin."

They headed toward the door. Once they got outside, she had that bad baby parked backwards. It was all white with tinted windows and some cute little wheels on it. Rika jumped in the passenger seat and laid her seat back while Faith popped in the new Anita Baker CD. They immediately started singing "No More Tears."

> *"We used to laugh, now all I do is cry. You used to make me happy, now you don't even try. You're hurting me and you're doing me wrong. I could see it in your eyes, soon you're going to be gone."*

This was the jam! They were popping their fingers and grooving to the music. Everything seemed to just vanish away. As much as Rika hated to admit it, she was glad she had made her way to see Faith. She was something special. It was different. They pulled up at Faith's Cousin Raven's house and Faith said they wouldn't be there long.

Raven had like five kids by four different baby daddies. But one thing Rika understood was Faith's cousin took good care of her kids. She made sure they had everything they needed and more. When Faith and Rika walked onto the porch, Faith didn't even bother to knock. They walked straight in and, of course, her cousin was in the kitchen doing what she did best (cooking).

"Hey, lady. What you been up to?" Faith asked her cousin Raven.

"Girl, nothing. Trying to get these kids fed so they can get out of my hair. Why? What you been up to? Hey, Rika. Long time no see. Last time I seen you, you was moving around at the party."

"Not a whole bunch," Rika replied. "Just trying to make it happen out here in these cold streets. You know what they say. 'When life gives you lemons, you make lemonade.'"

They all just fell out laughing.

"Girl, you still crazy. I'm miss your little butt though. You need to come over here so I can get you enrolled in school so you can do sumthin' with yo' self. Stop running around here acting like you don't have a care in the world. This is a cold, cold world out here and you got a baby. You need to just stop existing and start living!

"And, start being around people who really care about you," Raven continued. "Bitches you hang around don't give two fucks about you. Now I know you didn't come over here for me to give you a lecture, but you know me. I got mad love for you. I'm just trying to put some sense into your head. And, Rika, where's your baby at anyway?" She asked, turning to look Rika in her face.

Raven she was one of those real type of chicks. She was all about her kids, her man and her money. Family was everything to this woman, and every time they came in contact with each other, Rika learned something new. The problem was, she really didn't know how to use what she had given her because it was so much.

"She's with my mama," Rika replied.

"Well, Little Tyrone is having a birthday party this weekend. You should bring her. I don't want to hear no mess about your mama won't let you bring her, because I know she will. And, if you need me to, I will come pick you guys up."

"Naw, I will bring her," she said.

Rika knew her baby liked being around other kids, and she was looking forward to it. This would also be something that they could do together as mother and daughter. Faith, Raven and Rika sat back and had a few laughs, sipped on some Strawberry Hill Boone's Farm, and smoked a few blunts. No matter how messed up her life was, God always seemed to send genuine people around her that had her best interest at heart. It's funny how people can see the best in you when you can't even see it in yourself. That's what it was like being around Faith and Raven.

After eating and helping clean up the kitchen, Faith decided it was time to leave. Since she had the next few days off, her son was with his grandmother on his father's side, so she asked if

Rika wanted to spend the night at her house. Of course, Rika agreed. Faith knew Rika really didn't have anywhere to live, so (whenever she was off work) she made it a point to make sure that Rika was okay.

She took a shower and put on some clean clothes. Rika curled up in Raven's son's bed and just laid there thinking about what Raven said earlier. *How do you live? What does that mean? Rika* didn't even know the first steps to take. She didn't have any money, ID, nor did she have a plan. All she knew was the life she was living wasn't it. Rika knew, deep in her heart, that there was something better for her out there.

Rika didn't know what it was, but something in her wanted to fight. This wasn't just a physical fight, but this was a fight for her life. For the first time in a long time, she wanted to live. She wanted to be somebody. She was tired of using her body as a way of just getting by. She was tired of the every day hustle and bustle. She was tired of being used and mistreated. Rika was tired of being homeless. She was tired of being on drugs. Rika wanted to make something happen for herself. She didn't know where to start, but she knew she was tired of being tired and from that day forward she was about to do something about it.

Chapter Thirteen

Bentley's world was closing in on him. He learned that he couldn't go back to his old job at Taco Tico because the family of the young man he murdered had started watching his job and threatening his life because they knew that was where he worked. So, his job decided to transfer him to Kansas City, Missouri. That was cool because his auntie stayed there, and he knew he could always stay with her. Once he got there, he got a job at Gates & Sons Barbecue. Bentley loved his job. It was fun and nobody knew about his past. In a sense, you would say he felt free.

He knew he had to move quickly because Kameisha had just had their second child, Bentley III. So, he saved a few checks and sent for her and the kids. They stayed with his aunt for a while and, shortly after, moved into their own place. Things were looking up for his family, so he thought. Bentley didn't realize there was a warrant out for his arrest. After all the trouble that he had been in and his decision to move because of all the threats, his old landlord decided to take a few things out of Bentley's house. When Bentley found out, he took the man's tools. Unfortunately, he didn't realize that was considered theft.

One day, after he got off work, he was driving down Proctor Street and did not realize that he was in the turning lane. He kept straight and the police pulled him over, arrested him, and informed him that he had a governor's hold on him in Wichita, Kansas.

"What? Man, I haven't even been out there in a long time. Why are y'all arresting me?" He asked one of the police officers.

"Sir, get out of the car, please. You have to take this matter up with the judge. We're only doing our job," the cocky cop answered with his hand on his gun.

Bentley didn't even put up a fight. He just got out of the car and put his hands behind his back, and they escorted him to the backseat of the patrol car. Within four days, Wichita police expedited him back to Kansas to face the judge. The judge later lowered the charge to a misdemeanor. All Bentley could think about was, *This is some bullshit! Every time I turn around, they fucking with me. It seem like this shit will never end.*

Once again, Bentley was back in Wichita going through the same old stuff. After explaining the situation, he had his family moved back and they went to go live with Kameisha's mother. Bentley, on the other hand, spent a lot of time with Tonya. One day, after leaving Tonya's house, he went to QuikTrip on 13th & Oliver and ran into one of his old friends, Rahim.

"What's up? Boy, when did you get home?" Bentley asked, giving his old friend a manly hug.

"Man, I've been home for a few weeks now, trying to do to right thing. I ain't going back this time. I got too many kids out here to feed," Rahim said as he was eyeballing a shorty with some Daisy Dukes on.

"Man, I feel you. These police ain't playin' no games. What are you saying, a brother got too many mouths to feed? How many babies you got now?

"Six. Yeah, man. Six boys," Rahim said.

"Dang. You been working, huh? By your little high school sweetheart?" Bentley asked.

"Naw, by a chick from Louisiana. I don't think you know her. She from the sticks, and she know how to keep her man happy. As you can see, she spit me out six boys," he said and let out a hearty laugh.

They stood and talked for a few minutes, then they exchanged phone numbers and Bentley went his way. He knew he couldn't stay at QuikTrip too much longer because, with the life he lived, it was like the hotel and there was no telling who may rollup on him. Since his dad stayed right around the corner, Bentley decided to pay Flint a visit. When he pulled up in front of the house, his dad was outside watering the grass.

"Hey, dude. I thought you was in Kansas City," Flint said with a puzzled look on his face.

"Pops, man, the people just won't leave me alone."

Bentley explained everything to his father. And as much as he felt like he was a man, at this point, he felt just like a little boy wishing his father could help him with some of these emotions that he was feeling. Although they talked about a lot of things, how Bentley really felt, he never could share with his father. He felt like he had to be somebody that he wasn't in order to get his father's approval.

There were times Bentley would even ask Precious if his father even loved him. Because, when it came time to be there for his football games and any other sports that he played, his father was too busy posted up with other women and he left that job to Precious. This was no different. How could he tell his father that he was emotionally drained, and just needed to have a real heart-to-heart with somebody?

No matter how many people Bentley surrounded himself with, he never trusted anybody enough to share his true feelings. He didn't believe anybody could handle how he was really feeling because there were often times he couldn't handle how he was feeling himself. Over the next few months, Bentley spent a lot of time going from Tonya's to Kameisha's house (and a few other women in between). This was all he knew.

He and Rahim seemed to get closer and started to hang out more frequently. Although he said he had six boys, Bentley never saw them. Neither had he ever been to Rahim's house. Rahim seemed to be a little secretive about where he laid his head, but that didn't bother Bentley too much because that was the street code. You never let too many people know where you rest your head. So, he didn't pushed the issue.

It was hotter than heck outside, and Bentley was laid up in the house with Tonya when her phone rang.

"Hello," she answered in a soft voice.

"Is Bentley around?" The caller asked.

"May I ask who's calling?" She inquired.

"Is he there?" The caller asked, now getting irritated by all the questions.

Bentley looked at her with the crooked face and mouthed, "Who is it?" She shrugged her shoulders, as if to say, "I don't know."

So, he snatched the phone and said, "Hello, who is this?"

"Damn, man. You got your pit bull screening your phone calls?"

Rahim laughed. For some reason, Bentley didn't think it was funny. His question was, *How did you get this number?* But, he played it cool and looked over at Tonya with a puzzled look and fury in his eyes.

"I need to holler at you. Meet me at Spruce Park."

"What's going on?" Bentley asked, sounding nonchalant.

The truth was, he was irritated. He didn't understand. *For a person to be so private with his whereabouts and where he laid, how in the hell did he find out my whereabouts?* This was a problem for Bentley, but he played it cool.

"Yeah, man. What time you want to meet up there?"

"In about 30 minutes."

"I'll be there."

They hung up the phone. Now, Tonya was standing there shook-up like a snitch at a gangsta party because she didn't know how he had gotten her number. Something in her heart let her know that something wasn't right, and she wanted to warn Bentley. But, from the look on his face, she wasn't taking no chances. She was just going keep her mouth shut. Bentley was enraged. He grabbed Tonya by her throat and pushed her against the wall.

"If I find out you're messing around with this dude it's going be problems."

He gave her a hard shove and walked into the bathroom to take a shower. Tonya was stunned. She couldn't believe it. All she could do was cry. When Bentley exited the shower, he got dressed and left, slamming the door so hard that it shook the pictures on her wall. By the time he made it to Spruce Park, Rahim was sitting on the hood of his car with his music blasting.

"What's so important that I had to meet you here so fast?" Bentley asked as he got out of his car.

Rahim sensed his attitude, so he tried to make light of it, "Man, why are you acting like a little bitch, walking up here pouting."

Rahim was laughing so hard at his own joke that he didn't realize he had pissed Bentley all the way off.

"Look, nigga, don't you ever come at me like that again. First of all, how did you get my girl's number?"

He stood with his arms folded.

"Now, we're getting somewhere. You mad because I called your girl's house. Well, how else was I supposed to get a hold of you? You gave me your Pop's phone number, and every time I called there, your mom said you're not there. So, I took it upon myself to find out where you lay your head."

Rahim knew he was getting to Bentley. One night when they were hanging out, Bentley called Tonya from his phone and he knew he could use it for future reference, so he locked it in his phone. Bentley was so mad, he couldn't even comprehend what Rahim was saying to him. So, he just got right down to business.

"Okay, so now what. We here so what was so important?"

"I got this lick that I have lined up, and I need some help. I figured you needed some money in your pockets, and so do I. Are you down or what?" Bentley was a lot of things, but a jacker wasn't one of them. Yes, he could use the money in his pockets, but there were certain things that he wouldn't do to get it. Bentley calmed down at this point.

"I don't know man. That's not my line of work," he said, shaking as head.

"Man, this is simple as taking candy from a baby. You see, it's these dudes that's down here from Los Angeles and they got a shipment in. One of their homeboys is who' setting everything up. All you have to do is drive the car and, boom, you got about five or six grand in your pockets."

Rahim could see Bentleys wheels turning. And right before he could open his mouth, a little red Volkswagen Rabbit pulled up with tinted windows. There was a woman driving and, from the looks of it, there were some kids in the backseat. Bentley couldn't make out their faces from the distance he was standing. Rahim motioned for him to hold on as he walked up to the car.

Bentley couldn't determine what they were talking about, but he could tell they were arguing. Rahim hit the top of the Volkswagen and the woman driver sped off driving very reckless. By the time Rahim got back to where Bentley was standing, his whole attitude had changed.

"Everything alright, man?"

"Yeah, just some home-front issues but nothing that I can't handle. So, what's up? Are you in? It's simple."

"Let me think about it for minute because I do need some cash, and the way things have been going these last few months, that will put me right where I need to be. But I don't know. I feel like whatever the next man do to get what he has, I can do the same thing. So, that's never been my M.O."

He could tell that Rahim was getting irritated with him, but he didn't care. He gave Rahim dap and told him he would hook up with him in a few days to let him know what he was going to do. They gave each other a friendly handshake and a hug, and Bentley turned to walk back towards his car. What he didn't notice was the deadly look that Rahim gave him as he was turning his back.

I'm going to get you, nigga, if it's the last thing I do, Rahim thought to himself, while rubbing his hands together.

Chapter Fourteen

Rika had been thinking real hard about what Raven had said to her a few weeks ago. And, now that she'd found out her mother had moved with her daughter to Wichita, she knew she had to think quick. She knew she had to make a move of some kind. So, over the next few days, Rika began to think of what all she wanted to do in life. Although some of her thoughts were unrealistic, she did not rule anything out.

While she was visiting her daughter in Covina, California, that day Queen told her they were going to move, Rika decided to ask her mother to help her get her ID. Queen gave her all the information that she needed, and she handed her a $100 bill and told her where to go. Rika was so excited to finally be moving in the right direction, by the time she got to the DMV, she started smiling wide. She stood in those long lines until the process was completed.

After showing Queen her ID and telling her all the dreams and goals that she had, Queen was excited for Rika. To celebrate her new adventure and Queen's soon-to-be new location, Queen decided to take them to the In & Out Burger located right down the street on Irwindale Highway. Rika spent a few more days with her mother and Nila, and decided it was time for her to head back to the city to check on a few things and a few people. Her first stop was Wanda's house.

Rika hadn't seen Wanda for a while. Every since that situation happened with her and Bomb, Rika thought it would be a good idea to go and get some answers to what was really going on. It was a long ride on the bus from Covina to L.A. They were making all kinds of pit stops along the way, and there was some young girls on the bus talking so loud and acting so immature. Then, there was the drunk man in the back of the bus asking everybody that got on if he could have a quarter.

There was a young Mexican girl who was sitting in the front. It seemed she had just gotten home from school, because she had her backpack and a crying baby in her lap. Rika couldn't wait to get off the bus. As soon as her stop came up on Florence and Manchester, she almost broke her ankle trying to get off. As she walked down 75th Street and looked up at Wanda's apartment, she noticed her blinds were open.

As she got closer, the smell of Pine-Sol was coming through the windows. Rika knew she was up cleaning. The closer she got, she could hear her bumping "It Takes Two" by Rob Base and DJ EZ Rock. Shoot, Rika started grooving on the porch while she knocked on the door. Wanda didn't answer at first because the music was so loud. But finally Rika saw her peek through the window and, next thing she knew, she heard Wanda unlocking the screen door.

With excitement in her voice, Wanda said, "Hey girl, where the hell have you been?"

Wanda gave Rika a big long hug. They just stood in the door rocking and hugging each other.

"Dang. What's been up with you? It was as if you fell off the face of the earth," Wanda said, now backing away from the door to let Rika come all the way in.

"Nothing, just trying to get my head on straight," Rika said. "I smell it. Let me inhale it!"

They laughed like old times. She went in the kitchen and got her can from on top of the refrigerator and handed it to Rika. Rika knew just what to do with it, roll up. She sat down at the kitchen table and rolled up two fat ones -- one for her and one for Wanda.

"What's been going on? Why are you so excited? It's written all over your face, so share the good news," Wanda said, giving Rika a once-over.

Wanda was the freak of the bunch, so it didn't bother Rika that Wanda was prancing around in her booty shorts with no bra or panties on as if she was expecting someone. They all had gotten used to her attire, so they didn't say nothing else about it. They just let her be her and do whatever was she wanted to. Not to mention, this was her house and if Rika didn't like it all she had to do was leave.

But, this was her homegirl. They went way back. Rika didn't care that people called her names like whore, slut, and dick sucker. She was still her friend because Rika knew she had a good heart. Her only problem with her was, when she was around certain people, she acted a certain way -- as if she didn't know her own identity.

"Girl, I finally got my ID. I'm thinking about going back to school. I want to be a journalist. You know, being in the people business."

They cracked up laughing.

"You know, you will be a good one too because you stay in people business," Wanda joked.

"Naw, get it right. People put me in their business," Rika said as she blew out a cloud of smoke.

"Well, yeah. You're right about that. One thing I will say is you know how to keep shit to yourself. I've told you a whole lot of stuff, and I've never heard you repeat it."

"Speaking of keeping shit to myself, what was that all about between you and Jelly?"

"I knew you were going to ask. Listen, we have been creeping for a long time. I was messing with him first and I told Bomb that, but she tried to act like she didn't remember and then threatened to do something to me if I kept messing with him. So, a few weeks before that, Bomb and Jelly had got into a big fight and Bomb said I bet not tell nobody or she would look bad. What she really meant was don't tell you. For some reason, Bomb got a thing when it comes to you. I can't put my finger on it, but it's something.

"I've been wanting to tell you, but you seem not to want to listen to people when they tell you stuff about her. I think it's time for you to start paying attention, she's up to something. What it is, I don't really know. All I know is, when we are out and about making moves and your name comes up in the conversation, it's almost like horns stick out of her head. There's a lot that I want to tell you, but I don't know how you're going to process the information. What I will say is keep your eyes open, and just sit back and watch. Stop getting so drunk around her, because making a fool out of yourself only makes her look good. If you ask me, I would think she's a little jealous of you," Wanda continued.

"Now I know you may think you don't have nothing for a person to be jealous of, but one thing I have learned through the years is you don't have to have material things for a person to be jealous of you. It could just be who you are, like your personality and your inner strength. See, these are the things that you possess and the street didn't give that to you. That's a gift. All I'm saying is protect yourself and what's inside your heart. Don't let life make you cold and bitter. That's what's wrong with Bomb."

And, with that, Wanda took a long drag off her blunt and they changed the subject. It wasn't too far from Rika's mind though. All she kept thinking was, *Bomb is jealous of me? She can't be. Rika* thought Bomb had it going on. But, this went back to a lot of conversations that she had with her mother about people, and how they look good on the outside but their insides were contaminated.

She would often tell Rika, "Baby, jealousy is crueler than the grave. And, what's more cruel than that? Cement block. Cold, quiet and dead."

Wow! Queen always said she didn't trust Bomb and for Rika to be careful around her. It was that moment, sitting in that chair, Rika decided to leave and move to Wichita with her family. There was nothing in California for her anymore. She had partied and kicked it enough for a few generations. Robbing, trying to gangbang, using drugs, you name it and Rika's tried it. She didn't know if it was the marijuana or just her senses, but she knew she had to do something and do it quick. Because, in all true reality, she was on a mission to self-destruct. And, if the devil has his way, that is going to happen sooner than Rika thinks.

Chapter Fifteen

It had been a few weeks since her conversation with Wanda. And even though she listened to her, Rika really didn't hear what she said. She still kept her relationship with Bomb, but she did notice a few things about her that she wouldn't have if it wasn't for their conversation. Bomb was a hateful, mean bitch! It wasn't just Rika she was jealous of, it was anybody that had a desire to live. Rika also noticed that all of Bomb's conversations glorified herself to make others feel low. She would sell out her own soul if it made her look good, and that wasn't a good sign.

It was as if her intuition had started to kick in. It was almost as if the scales had fallen of her eyes and Rika was becoming aware of her self-worth, but not fully. She still saw this broken woman that needed some help, so Rika tolerated her. It was then that the fear that Rika had for Bomb wasn't a natural fear, but a spiritual fear. Bomb was lost and wasn't trying to be found. She had allowed herself to become her own god. And, from what Rika knew about God, that's a very dangerous place to be, and until she made it right with Him, nobody stood a chance.

Rika walked in Carima's house and she was sitting on the couch. As soon as she saw Rika, the first thing out of her mouth was, "Your momma been looking for you."

"What?" Rika said flopping down on the couch right next to her.

"Yeah, she's been calling everyday. I told her I would have you call her whenever you decided to drop by," Carima said as she dialed the number and handed the phone to Rika.

It rang a couple of times before Queen answered, "Hello."

"Hi, Mommy."

"Hi, baby. How are you?"

"I'm okay. How about you?"

"Good. Good. Your baby has been asking about you, and you know how she gets when she's ready to see you. I just wanted to know, if you want to come down here."

"That fine. When?"

"Whenever you want to, just tell me and I will send you a ticket."

That was music to Rika's ears. Hell, she didn't know if Queen could hear the excitement in her voice, but Carima saw it on her face. Carima knew the whole time what Queen wanted, but she wanted her to tell Rika.

"I don't care. You just tell me when and I'll leave," Rika said.

"How about tomorrow?" Queen asked.

At first, Rika hesitated. "Tomorrow?"

Then she thought, *Fuck it*! *I don't have nothing to lose. Why not.* "That's fine," she said.

Rika could hear Queen smiling through the phone.

"You know your brother, Meeka and the kids are here."

That was cool, at least there would be some familiar faces and Rika wouldn't feel so out of place. She started to get super excited but afraid of the unknown at the same time. For the rest of the day, she packed what little she had and Carima made sure Rika didn't leave her sight. She made sure Rika had a hefty bag of goodies -- from fried chicken and sandwiches to fruit. You name it and she had it.

Rika didn't realize the bus ride was two days but, for her new beginning, it was worth it. By the time Rika arrived in Kansas, it was cold as heck! But the look on her mother's face was priceless! She hugged and kissed Rika, and it felt so right. This was the move that she was supposed to make.

"Where's Nila?"

"She's with Rodge. I wanted to surprise her. She doesn't know your coming."

Wichita seemed dull and dry, being that Rika was coming from the city. As they drove down Hillside, she noticed there were lots of cemeteries almost back to back. When they pulled up to Rodge's house, it was on a dead end next to some railroad tracks. Rika laughed to herself, remembering when Rodge and Meeka lived in the Pueblos literally right next to the tracks. Rodge must have seen Queen when she pulled up because they had the kids to go into their room for Rika to enter the house. As soon as she walked into the house, she gave Rodge a big hug. But, when it came to Meeka, they gave their signature greeting, which consisted of a big hug, kisses and tears.

"Y'all just can't live nowhere if tracks aren't involved, huh?" Rika said, and they all busted out laughing.

"Girl, tell me about it. When I first saw this place, I said the same thang," Meeka said.

Rika was enjoying all of this, but she wanted to see her little chocolate drop. She believes they all sensed it because her mother pointed to the room where the kids were playing. As Rika approached the room, she could hear them laughing and playing, so she eased the door open. At first Nila had a confused look on her face. Rika could tell when it registered in Nila's mind who Rika was because, in one swift jump, Nila leaped into her arms.

"Momma," she wailed.

"Hey, my baby."

They took a few minutes to just love on each other.

"When you come?" She asked in her little voice.

At the age of three, the doctors discovered that Nila was hard of hearing. Her speech was different, as well as her vocabulary. This made some of the things she said sound unique, and only those close to her could understand.

"Today, are you glad to see me?"

She nodded her little head, smiling showing off her little silver-capped teeth.

"You ride the big bus?"

"Yes, I rode the big bus."

Rika knew she was referring to the Greyhound. After spending about an hour talking to the family, her Uncle Frank walked in and Rika almost didn't recognize him. The last time she saw him, he was strung out on heroine and pushing a shopping cart on Vermont in L.A. Now, he was clean and sober, looking healthy and refreshed.

"Hey, Unc," she said, giving him a big hug.

Now, this was Queen's baby brother that she took care of like he was her own son. Rika found out that when Queen moved to Kansas, she brought Frank with her so that he could get clean and sober.

"Today marks a year that I've been sober. So, the center is giving a drug-free dance to celebrate everyone. Are y'all going to come?" Frank asked.

Rodge immediately dismissed that thought and volunteered Rika and Meeka. Meeka was down for the cause, so they got all the information so that they could be in attendance. With that being said, Queen decided that they should go home so Rika could get some rest and have some bonding time with Nila. When they finally arrived at her mother's house, which faced Hillside, Rika noticed that Queen lived directly across the street from another cemetery. That gave her the creeps.

All kinds of thoughts raced through Rika's head. But once their family was inside, it was as peaceful as could be. It was as if the cemetery didn't even exist. Rika didn't know why she was so surprised about how peaceful it was. Rika's mother was a praying woman, and everywhere they lived was just like that.

She showed Rika to her daughter's room, which was full of color and bears. She put her things down and Queen showed Rika the rest of the house, which was immaculate. They made their way to the kitchen with Nila leading the way. Rika noticed that Queen had made her favorites -- hot water cornbread, fried chicken, greens and jello. She was delighted!

"Are you tired?" Queen asked.

"No, not really. But I am glad to be off that greasy dawg though," Rika said.

They laughed. Over the next few hours, Rika played with Nila while her mother conducted some church business over the phone, and then decided it was time to get dressed to go help her uncle celebrate his sobriety.

Chapter Sixteen

Bentley had been dealing with all kinds of legal matters -- from burglary to domestic disputes and fighting. You name it, it was happening. After going to court for the burglary, they placed him in a facility called Community Corrections -- which is one step away from prison. That meant he had one foot on a banana peel and the other inside the prison door. Once again, he was in a fucked up situation that, for the life of him, he couldn't understand. He had to admit he had been wilding out for no apparent reason. To him, he had become a target for bullshit.

Why? Why do I always find myself in these predicaments? But he did what he always done, he blew it off and did what he did best, blocked it out. When he was done with all of the processing and given his bedding, he was escorted to his living quarters. He put his things down and went into the rec room where he realized that all his homies, and even a few family members, were there.

"What's up! What's up," his homeboys began to yell.

He received nothing but love from his fellow gang family and biological family. They talked for a few minutes before Bentley realized something seemed fishy. His homies were in the corner of the room and, from what he could hear, something wasn't right and they were plotting. Because Community Corrections wasn't a jail, you were allowed to have certain things -- like your own clothes, jewelry, and even your own car. By the time he tuned in, they were planning on going to a party later on that night, but the catch to it was they were only allowed to sign themselves out to go to different meetings.

One of the homies realized there was a drug-free dance later on that night. He said, since curfew was at midnight, they could slide to the dance, get their slip signed, and head to the Blood party that the Big Homie was giving. That was a plan, so they all signed up to go. Once they got it approved, their plans were in full motion.

On the way to the dance, everybody was hyped about the party. Bentley, on the other hand, was in his own thoughts. Bentley couldn't escape the four walls of his mind that seemed so dark and gloomy, emotionally and mentally. He was just drained. In his heart, he was not the person that was showing up on the outside. But, he had no clue on how to fix it. He knew that the justice system had given him multiple chances to get it right but, for some reason, he didn't know how to do that.

Once he began to think of mentors, or even positive role models, he had none. So, once again, he rejected his thoughts and tried to move forward. Before he knew it, they were pulling into the YMCA. They all exited the car. Bentley was fresh to death, rocking his tan Timberland boots with a burgundy vest, Dickies sagging off his waist, and his fat ass gold link chain around his neck. Shit, you couldn't tell him nothing. On the outside, he had it all together but, inwardly, he was a total mess. They entered the building about ten deep. The place was empty and dim. They looked around for the person in charge to get their slip signed so they could exit the building.

"Hey, umm, is Lisa Banister available?" One of the homies asked.

"She is. Are you here for the celebration?"

E-Rock thought to himself, *I don't know about a celebration but whatever*.

"Yes," he said, getting frustrated. "I'll tell her you're here, but for now you can enjoy some refreshments over there on the table while I page her."

They walked away without uttering another word and headed towards the area where the refreshments were. Bentley looked around, shaking his head with disgust until he spotted two women dancing in the corner. He said to himself, *It don't look like they belong here.*

They walked up to the refreshment table, grabbed a few drinks, and made their way to the bench to wait for Lisa to sign their slip so they could shake this joint. Bentley sat close enough to get a good look at the two women that no one else seemed to be paying attention to but, before he could focus in good, one of them headed in his direction. The closer she got, his nerves began to spiral out of control. He told himself to play it cool, so he decided to play shy.

"What's up link chain? You want to dance?" Rika asked.

"Naw, baby. I don't dance. This song is whack, maybe another song," he said, grabbing her hand so she could sit down beside him.

"Oh, okay," she said.

Before he could utter another word, she had gotten up and walked off. Rika resumed dancing with her friend. *Damn! What just happened?* Bentley wondered.

"Oh snap! You just got shot down," his boys started to tease.

"Never that, I'm just playing it cool. Don't worry. I got this," he assured them.

The next few songs were whack too. By this time, Lisa was coming to sign their slips so they could exit the building. They had to play it off so she wouldn't call CC and tell them that they had left. So, Bentley decided it was time to make his move. He had sat there long enough watching Rika make the music dance to her beat.

Her moves were so graceful and in control, not wild and all over the place. He even liked the outfit she wore, it was tasteful but slutty. He knew she wasn't from around there by the accent. He slowly walked up behind her with his entourage in tow and started moving to her beat.

"Oh. So you dance now, right?" Rika asked full of sarcasm.

"Naw, baby. That song was just whack."

She didn't pay him any attention because, the truth was, her and Meeka spotted them when they walked in and it was a bet to see if Rika would walk up and ask him to dance. Since they were there only for a brief moment, he asked her for her number and she walked him outside to his car.

"Can I have a kiss?" He asked.

"Boy bye!"

They laughed.

"I'm going to call you tomorrow," he said and the guys drove away.

On the way to their real destination, they shot the breeze about gang issues and things that needed to change. But, Bentley was still thinking about this mystery woman that he had just made contact with. Rika had revealed to him that she was out there from L.A., and she didn't know how long she would be in town. *The thing is, why was she at a drug-free dance?* Now that was puzzling.

They arrived at the party and everybody that was somebody was there. Once they were inside, the smell of weed filled the air, drinks were flowing, music was bumping, and everybody was having a good time. Over in the corner, couples were bumping and grinding. Bentley and his crew strolled through, giving different homies dap and saying what's-ups. They finally made it to the back where a crap game was in full swing. Rahim had the dice and, from the looks of it, he was putting a killing on them.

"Why the sour face? Y'all know what time it is. Shit. I got kids and a wife to feed," he said laughing and taunting them.

Big Rick was standing on the sidelines being a spectator. He wasn't trying to get in the game. The last time he rolled against Rah, he lost all his money. But he wasn't no punk about it. He had earned his name in these streets. The only reason he was on the sidelines was because there had been a lot of talk in theses streets about, "This nigga playing with the funny dice." If that was the case, tonight was his night to be handled.

Rah had his little sidekick with him making side bets, which was raising a lot of red flags in Big Rick's mind. He didn't say anything, but he was glued to the table watching Rah's every move. What the homies didn't know was Rick had a plan of his own. He brought his goons with him from Kansas City and they were just waiting for Big Rick to make any gesture that insinuated "game on."

They were strapped like Wells Fargo. Rah, on the other hand, wasn't asleep on the fact that these niggas were tight about all his winnings and he had some goons as well. The only difference was they weren't posted up around the crap game, they were spread throughout the party.

"What that hit fo?"

A voice came from out of nowhere. It was Tre, this dude from around the way.

"You gone have to wait yo' turn, young blood," somebody in the crowd responded.

For some reason, the atmosphere was very uncomfortable and the tension in the room could be cut with a knife. Bentley wasn't really feeling it and was really ready to leave, but his homies that he came with seemed to not be paying any attention to what was going on around them. All they were interested in was smashing one of these chicks. Big Rick was getting irritated because Rah was antagonizing them every time he rolled the dice.

"Show these clowns what time it is baby!" He laughed and blew on the dice.

"Nigga don't keep being disrespectful up in here. Shit, I gave you a pass at the crap table the other day. Don't get your fucking wig split," Big Rick exclaimed.

By this time, Rah got up from his knees real calm and stood directly in Big Rick's face and said, "My heart don't pump no Kool-Aid, bitch-ass nigga!"

By this time, everybody was at full attention. The homeboy's mom came from the back of the house when she heard all of the commotion.

"What the hell is going on in here? If anybody gone to be fighting in here, its going to be me! Now if y'all niggas can't get out of your feelings about loosing a penny or two, then you shouldn't be in the game period!"

By now, Big Rick and Rah were having a major stare down. Rah decided to take the low road, "Yeah, you right. It's cool. Whose roll is it?"

From the looks of things, he was trying to keep the peace, but no one even noticed the wink he gave to the dude standing over in the corner with the long ponytail. Big Rick calmed down too and was like, "You right, Moms. I'mma chill out, but don't no man pump fear in my heart. But I'm cool."

He headed to the bathroom. Once he got there, he noticed it was in use so he decided to go downstairs in the basement to see if that bathroom was occupied.

"Shit," he said as he bang on the door.

"I'm using it," a voice came from the other side of the door.

As he headed back up the stairs, Bentley and his crew were about to head out because their time was running short and they had to get back to CC, "You straight, Big Homie?" Bentley asked.

"I'm good. Where y'all off to?" Big Rick asked as everybody gave their signature handshake.

"Back to the doghouse."

They all laughed as they jumped in the car and sped off. Big Rick decided to take a leak on the side of the house. Just as he was releasing himself, someone came out of the darkness with one swift motion.

Boom! Boom! Boom!

That was it. He fell face first in his urine. He was dead before he even hit the ground. Just as fast as the dude with the ponytail came, he left.

Chapter Seventeen

Rika woke up to the phone ringing off the hook. Her head was pounding from the hangover she had. It was Sunday morning, so Rika knew Queen was at church. Rika ran down the stairs to answer the phone.

"Hello," she answered.

"Hi. Is Rika available?" The voice on the other end asked.

"Yes, this is Rika," she said, looking around puzzled.

"This is Bentley, the guy you met last night."

Rika's head was spinning. She could vaguely remember what Bentley looked like. Although it was a drug-free dance, she was as drunk as a skunk. *Hell, they didn't say no alcohol.*

"Hi, how are you?" Rika asked, looking down at little Nila while she played in her hair.

They talked for about thirty minutes and had made plans for him to come by and see Rika. Rika was a little nervous because she really couldn't remember how he looked. All she remembered was that he smelled good as heck. By the time Queen came home from church, she had gotten Nila and herself dressed and warmed up the food that Queen had cooked the day before.

"How was church?" Rika asked.

"It was good. You know the Lord showed up and we had a time," Queen began to repeat the entire message almost word for word.

One thing about it, she loved God and she wanted all her babies to be saved. She would often preach to them when they were young.

"Now if y'all going to go to hell, you might as well go first class. Ain't no need of you sitting in church and still going to hell. If you don't do nothing else, go to church for safety sake. I'm not telling y'all to join the church or to get saved, but honor God. Give Him what's due Him," she would stress.

One thing about it, God had given her wisdom. She knew that if they kept going for "safety sake," God was going to do the rest. Rika would often say to herself, *God knows my heart*, and, in all reality, He did. He knew that her mind was full of corruption and she had no desire to run around being a hypocrite, so she would be lying to herself to say anything different. But Rika was about to learn, real quick, that you can't hold hands with the devil and God at the same time.

"Mommy, I met someone last night at the dance and he wants to now if he can stop by," Rika asked.

She just simply said, "Sure," and went to her room to change clothes. About an hour later, Bentley pulled up in a two-toned Pontiac with tinted windows. It took him a minute to get out of the car, so Rika just sat in the window waiting to see what he really looked like because she was too drunk the night before to even notice. When he finally exited the car, she was stunned. He was a smooth dude with a caramel complexion, and he stood about 5'6" with bowlegs. He had on a nice pair of creased shorts, which hung off his hips just right and were a perfect indication that he had some thug in him (just the way Rika liked it). By the time he climbed the steps to ring the doorbell, she had already swung the door open.

"Hello," Rika said, walking outside to meet him and also stopping him from entering the house.

"What's up," he responded with a smile.

The first thing she noticed was his deep dimple on his right cheek. When she looked into his eyes, they were a hazel color and they stared right back at her. It was that moment that Rika thought something that she never thought before in her life. *He's mine. This is going to be my husband.* For the next few hours, they sat on the porch laughing and talking while they watched Nila play in the yard. The conversation went very well.

"Do you gang bang?" Rika asked out of no where, even though she already knew the answer.

"Yeah," he said.

"Okay. Whatever you do, don't say that to my mother," she warned.

"Why not?"

"Just don't."

Before the words could get out of her mouth good, Queen came out of the house. She greeted him and gave him a quick look over.

"Hi, I'm Queen," she said, extending her hand.

"I'm Bentley, and how are you?" He sounded so polite.

"Are you from around here?" Queen asked.

"Yes, I was born and raised here," he replied.

"Are you a gang member?" She asked him.

Before Rika could even turn her head to give him that reminder look, he had already responded, "Yes I am."

Rika thought she was going to pass out. Rika knew Queen wasn't game goofy, but Rika didn't want him to tell her for some weird reason.

"I know. I could look at you and tell," Queen said.

With that, she took Nila in the house to get her out of the heat. Rika looked at him like, "Didn't I tell you not to say anything?"

He answered her thoughts, by saying, "For some reason I couldn't lie to her."

She knew it was her spirit that made it where he couldn't lie to her, so Rika gave him a pass that time. They sat there for a little while longer before he had to go. She didn't quite understand why he was on a time schedule, and she didn't question it either. They said their good-byes and he left.

Over the next few months, they had become really close. She decided to get a job and stay in Kansas not because of him, but for the simple fact that Rika thought she could do better there because it was a slower pace. One thing about life, it doesn't matter where you move, some demons must be left behind before true change can began in your life.

One weekend, Bentley called her up and invited her to a party.

"Hey! I am going to pick you up in a little while so we can roll to this party my homies are giving," he said.

Now, Rika was a little confused because he could never be out late because the aunt that he was living with didn't allow him to come in her house after a certain time.

So, Rika asked him, "Is your aunt going to let you in the house if you come in too late?"

"Yeah, she will. I talked to her about it already," he lied.

"Oh, okay, I'll see you soon," Rika said.

Rika hung up the phone and started laying her clothes out. Things were going very well so far. Not only was Rika working two jobs, but she was also moving into her own place in a few days. Bentley picked her up for the party around 9 p.m. They stopped at the liquor store, grabbed a couple of 64-ounce bottles of Old English 800, and a few cigarillos so she could roll some blunts because he didn't smoke. They headed straight to the party. Outside of the drug-free dance, Rika hadn't been anywhere entertaining.

They pulled up at this house that sat on a hill. While sitting in the car rolling her blunt and drinking her beer right out of the bottle, Rika watched all kinds of people coming and going. For some reason, she was very uncomfortable because some dudes were wearing red and some in blue. This was very different from the streets where she come from. It was either one color or the other, period. They finally jumped out of the car and walked up to the house. Once they got inside, the music was extremely loud, all the lights were on, and people were just sitting around talking amongst themselves. Bentley introduced her to a few fellas and some females. He grabbed her hand and led her to the kitchen where some more dudes were drunk and talking shit.

"What's down, Big Homie?" The drunkest dude of them all slurred.

"What's down, blood?" Bentley replied.

"What's down, blood?" He said to another cat that had stared Rika down from the moment they entered the kitchen.

"Rah, this is my girl, Rika. Rika, this is Rahim."

"Hello," he said as nice as possible.

Rika quickly turned her head and looked the other way because his eyes were dark and cold.

She knew that he wasn't right. She couldn't quite put her finger on it, but she knew he was bad news.

Chapter Eighteen

Things with Bentley and Rika seemed to be going pretty smooth so far. Rika was as cool as a fan and Bentley was digging her for the most part. He had finally met her brother Rodge, and that cat was as gangsta as they came. Bentley knew Rika had to have some hood in her even though she kept trying to play the role like she didn't. He knew she wasn't keeping it all the way real with him. He figured some things were better left unsaid. On the flip side of the coin, Bentley's legal matters had gotten ten times worse after talking to Rah about them putting him in Community Corrections.

"Man, please. That's some bullshit! Ain't no way in hell they could make me stay in no shit like that. If I was you, homie, on the for real, I'd get up out that bitch. What can they really do? Shit, you come and go pretty much as you please already anyway, right?" Rahim said, trying to convince him.

"Yeap, some what," Bentley said.

"Well fuck 'em! They can't do shit. You got somewhere to rest your head at. Don't you? You still with Fatima right?"

"Yeap," Bentley said, really thinking about what Rah was presenting to him.

He made it sound so good and convincing that Bentley never weighed out all the consequences that he, and only he, would be facing.

"Oh yeah, and another thing. That bitch that you brung to the party the other night. Who was she?" Rah began to question.

"First off, she ain't no bitch. That's my chick. What about her?"

Now, Bentley was getting real tight, and even he didn't understand why.

"Calm down, nigga. All I'm trying to tell you is you better watch out for her. For some reason, I don't like her at all. I get this bad vibe about her. All I'm saying is be careful."

They discussed some future business and they each went their separate ways. Bentley eventually took his advice and left CC, but what he wasn't prepared for was the "aggravated escape from custody" warrant they put out for his arrest. *What the fuck!* He thought to himself when Fatima delivered the news about the police surrounding their house one morning she was leaving for work.

"What did they say?" He asked, shaking his head in disbelief.

"Nothing, they want you to turn yourself in," Fatima delivered the news.

Fatima was someone who Bentley met right before Kameisha lied and moved to New York with his kids. They had been together for years now. Bentley cared for her, but he wasn't in love with her. He knew, eventually, he had to move around but, for now, she was considered his main chick.

"Why the hell did you leave in the first place?" She wanted to know.

"Man, I don't know. But, I damn sure didn't think they were going to hit me with no shit like this," he said.

Once again, Bentley was in deep shit with the laws, and those same old feelings of defeat had set in. When a person feels defeated, they become very reckless to themselves and others.

"I can't win for losing," he began to prophesy to himself.

He decided that he needed to pay Rika a visit. She seemed to be his safe haven these days. Just being around her and her family brought some form of peace and life. He couldn't get to her fast enough. Once he got up to the porch, all he saw was her and Nila charging him. Rika jumped in his arms and gave him a big kiss on his cheek. Not one time did she say how much she missed him, but she expressed it through her actions. After feeling the love she had for him, he knew he made the right choice to go see her.

"What are you doing tonight?" Rika asked him.

"Nothing, why what's up?"

"You should come to church with me tonight."

This caught him way off guard, and he said yes before he knew it.

"Great! My mother always recommend that we go for safety sake, so now you can practice this same principle," Rika said.

Bentley didn't know what he had gotten himself into, but he knew he had to keep his end of the deal. That night when they arrived at church, he was listening to the minister preach about somebody named Abraham, and how he had faith enough to sacrifice his own son. Bentley thought this was bizarre. *Whoever this God was that gave him a baby was now asking him to sacrifice him?*

Bentley was lost. *This is not the same God that everybody talk about is it? How can he give somebody something and then turn around and ask you to kill it? Man, please.* And just when he was about to dismiss every word he had just heard, out of all the people that were in the church (and I mean it had to be about 200 people), this dude picked Bentley to come to the front of the church. He looked over and saw Queen smiling and motioning him to go on, so he walked to the front.

To make things more intriguing, the preacher made Bentley come all the way on the pulpit and gave him a big hug in front of everybody. If Bentley were white, he would have been as red as a beet. Bentley was nervous and didn't know what to think about this man whom he had never met hugging on him in front of all these folks. Although he was nervous, he felt some kind of peace at the same time.

After church, they went back to Queen's house and sat on the porch. He wanted to ask Rika to explain what happened, but he didn't want to sound stupid. He could hear Rah in his mind, *"It's something about her."* Bentley began to get uncomfortable.

Yeah, they might be devil worshippers or something. Let me get the fuck up out of here. With that, he was out. He made it a point to keep his distance from Rika for a while. He started hanging out with Rah and his homeboy. One day, Rah finally invited Bentley to his house that he shared with his wife and sons. When he arrived, Rah opened the door and let him in. Once inside, Bentley felt extremely heavy, as if he had weights on his ankles. He immediately became hot and irritated. Rah must have sensed something.

"You alright, man?"

"Yeah, I'm cool," Bentley said, trying to regain his composure.

No-one else in the house seemed to be affected by this demanding atmosphere. He quickly tried to get it together when Rah's wife walked up and handed him a glass of ice water.

"Thank you," he said, reaching for the glass.

She didn't reply. In fact, she didn't even make eye contact. It was almost like she was looking right through him. Rah caught the puzzled look on Bentley's face and cleaned it up real quick.

"I run my house man, and women stay in their places around here," he said.

Everybody started laughing, including Bentley. He was starting to feel a little bit better, but the heaviness wouldn't seem to go away. They sat around and watched the football game, with the Kansas City Chiefs taking the victory. Everybody seemed to be enjoying themselves. Rah was in his glory talking shit to his homeboys, making them feel like nobodies. But that wasn't what caught Bentley's attention.

He couldn't help but notice this dude with a long ponytail going in and out of one of the back rooms. He never interacted with the rest of the guys that were watching the game. In fact, he had this weird distorted look on his face as he watched Bentley every time he came out of the room.

Bentley decided he had enough. Something was draining the life right out of him. The longer he sat there, the more he was being controlled by this atmosphere. He had never been a hateful, bitter, or self-destructing person. But, for some reason, his mind began to go in areas he had never been before.

Once he got outside to his car, he looked back at the house. Staring at him from one of the room windows was Rah's wife. For the first time, Bentley got a good look at her. Even though she was gorgeous, a feeling of hurt and sadness ripped through Bentley's heart. In a flash, it seemed like someone or something snatched her out of the window.

Chapter Nineteen

Time was moving very quickly, and it seemed like Bentley had fallen victim to his circumstances. He was starting to feel like his world was caving in on him and everything that could go wrong was. Not only was he sitting in the county jail waiting for sentencing, but his relationship with Rika was at a standstill. He found himself drinking more than normal, and taking things out on her that didn't have anything to do with her.

As he sat in jail, he began to replay the last few weeks of his freedom and how he began to hurt the people that truly loved him. Bentley thought about how he felt like he had lost control of his life in a matter of weeks. He tried his best to shake people that he had convinced himself were no good for him, only to find out that he was isolating himself from reality.

Precious had noticed the change in him and tried to reason with him. She told him that he needed to change the people he was hanging out with.

"I'm not used to you being so down and out. Have you talked to the kids since they left?" She asked with much concern in her voice.

Precious knew something was wrong with her son, but she didn't know how to help him. He was heading in a direction that could only lead to two places, jail or death. The only time he seemed happy was when he was with his dad or when he would bring Rika around. Precious knew Rika was good for Bentley because, even though she was a sweet young lady, there were some things that she too was struggling with.

"Yes, I talked to them. Kameisha wants me to move to New York, but I ain't going down there. She will never get me up there and have me lynched," Bentley said.

Bentley had begun to hate Kameisha for leaving with his kids, not really looking at his own faults and what caused her to really leave. The saying is true, hurt people hurt other people -- whether it be physically, mentally or emotionally. One of the things that he never saw in himself was how selfish he was. When you are around people and they're doing the same thing that you are doing, it becomes your normal.

After watching Flint treat Precious the way he did, and she was still there over 20 years later, Bentley felt like this was the normal thing to do (abuse women). What was never revealed to him was, when you lay down at night, you find yourself being restless and constantly looking over your shoulders (running from your own demons). Creed said it best in "My Own Prison" when he wrote:

A court is in session, a verdict is in.
No appeal on the docket today.
Just my own sin.

When you're living a life of deceit and manipulation, you're only chaining yourself down in the walls of your own mind. Bentley was about to learn sooner than he was expecting how quickly the tables turn when you're trapped in your four walls.

Rika was starting to feel herself falling back into her old ways of life and thinking. She had started back smoking crack on the low because she knew it would have just killed Queen and Nila to find out she had relapsed after she was doing so well. She also had started back to talking to her crew in L.A. Bomb was still up to her same old lies and schemes, trying to convince Rika that she wasn't really happy and that she was still a nobody. As much as Rika knew that was a lie, for some reason she found truth in what Bomb was saying.

"You way down there, and you still can't keep no man. How long has it been since you found out he was married, with five kids and living with a woman you thought was his aunt?" She taunted. "Girl, please, you could have stayed here for that bullshit you going through, and you got the nerve to say you've been praying? To who? Because, God ain't listening apparently. And, besides, He don't listen to sinners. That's why I have been trying to show you, praying only works when it comes to your momma and the rest of them old folks in your family. You have done too much for Him to listen to you. If I were you, I would cut my losses with that God stuff, and just do you."

Bomb's words echoed in Rika's head. And, for some reason, she began to believe what Bomb was saying. *Shoot!* Rika had been fasting for over 30 days for her and Bentley to get married, and that hadn't happened yet. She had also asked God to make her serve Him, and again nothing had happened yet. In fact, things began to get worse since she began to fast and pray.

"Hold on for a minute, my other line is ringing," Bomb announced.

"Hello," she answered in a sexy voice.

"What's good cousin?" A familiar voice boomed from the other end.

"Hey now! Not a whole lot. I haven't heard from you in decades. Whatchu got for me?" She teased the caller on the other end.

"Ahh, just some work that needs your touch. I'm gonna need you to come take care of something for me in a few weeks. And, I'm going to need you to be ready with your game face on when I give you the word," the person instructed.

"What's in it for me?" Bomb asked, getting in full destruction mode.

"You know I got you. But, no! This won't be as simple as the other jobs you've done for me. If you pull this one off, we can take a lot of suckas down with us. Be ready when I give the word."

With that, the caller hung up and Bomb knew that this was a serious one because she could hear the urgency in her cousin's voice. Bomb clicked back over and said, "I gotta go, but don't forget what I said. Leave that church stuff alone. It's not for you. Do what I taught you. 'Get it how you live.'"

And with that, she hung up. Rika sat in her living room thinking of what that meant for her, when she heard a small still voice say:

> Before I formed thee in the belly I knew
> thee; and before thou camest forth out of
> the womb I sanctified thee, and I ordained
> thee a prophet unto the nations.
> (Jeremiah 1:5 KJV)

She was startled because the voice sounded like it was coming from right next to her. She thought to herself, *Was God speaking to me?* She began to weep and cry out. Even though she didn't feel worthy of His presence, she felt His peace.

Almost instantly, a breeze came through her front door, giving her a calm feeling. She wanted to surrender to the feelings that were rushing through her body, but the words Bomb had spoken to her almost minutes earlier caused her fear. And, not just any kind of fear, but that paralyzing fear which creates a stronghold in your mind. Rika shook it off and blamed it on the blunt that she was smoking.

God wouldn't speak to me. I'm too low down for Him. She laughed out loud. *I mean, look at me. I'm a drug addicted, fornicating, lustful, pitiful mess. Why would God want any dealing with me? I'm a straight fuck up. Hell, my own mother don't like fooling with me at times, and I came from her. So, why would God?*

Rika jumped up and went to get in the shower. She got out of the shower and moisturized her body with Skin-So-Soft and got ready for bed. As soon as she was about to dose off into that deep sleep, she felt a warm presence enter her room. Since she was there by herself, fear raced through her body and she jumped up. But just as silent as it entered, it left.

Okay. I'm tripping, she thought to herself. She knew she had a long day ahead of her, but she was also excited because she found out that Bentley was in the county jail and she was going to go see him. With that in mind, she smiled herself to sleep anticipating their reunion.

Chapter Twenty

Bentley went back to his pod feeling ecstatic. Earlier that day, the judge had reinstated his probation for another year so, in a few more hours, he would be a free man. To top that, he was just visited by Rika. After seeing her, he knew there was no one and nothing that would stop him from marrying her once he got himself together. But, before he could do anything, he had to handle some serious business.

While he was in the county for those few weeks, the jailhouse began to talk and confirm some things that he had been feeling. One night when he was sleeping, he saw a vision of someone trying to destroy him. He couldn't put a face on the person because it was too dark for him to make out the person's face. But this person was trying to kill everyone around him, including those that Rika loved the most -- and she happened to be his number one target. *But why?* Bentley thought. *Why would she be of any importance to this big giant. She is a woman. Shit, why didn't he want to fight me?*

Bentley got mad hands and, in his vision, he was squirming, trying to get the full gist of things. But every time he tried to move, he realized he was shackled by a force greater than himself. As bad as he wanted to help, he couldn't. As he began to look around for something, anything, to free himself, he noticed blood and mass amounts of it. He traced where it was coming from when he realized that he was wounded and badly. Bentley struggled with all his might to free his hands once he heard Rika scream for his help.

"Grrrrrrrrr!" He yelled.

Bentley finally got one of his hands out of the ropes, which took everything out of him. Defeat set in once again, but this time Bentley said out loud, "God help me!" Once again, he heard the words of Creed:

A light to free me from my burden.
And grant me life eternally.

At that moment, he felt light. And just as he began to run in the direction where the people took Rika, he saw a guy in the distance with a long ponytail running. That was when it all started to make sense. Rah was behind everything -- him going to jail, his breakups with Tonya and Fatima, and now he was trying to destroy his relationship with Rika. Now, that was where he fucked up. After Bentley went over countless conversations in his mind that he had with Rah, his blood began to boil.

This nigga been playing me this whole time, even when we were youngsters. But, why? I thought we were better than that? I know he felt some kind of way about me getting with Tonya, but she said it wasn't nothing between them. That's when it hit Bentley. *This clown is salty about something and I'm going to get to the bottom of it once and for all.*

By the time they let Bentley out of the county jail, Rika was there to greet him with open arms. As glad as he was to see her, he needed to be by himself. He needed to come up with a plan and he didn't need any distractions. But, he would play it cool for now.

"Hi there, mister?" Rika said.

"Aww, you know, just trying to keep my head above water."

They both laughed. On the ride home, they made small talk, but Rika could tell something was weighing heavy on Bentley's mind.

She asked, "What's wrong baby? And, don't say nothing either."

He looked at her, trying to feel her out for real to see if he could trust her with some of his deepest thoughts. Although he was feeling some kind of way about Rah, he had warned Bentley to watch Rika. So, he had conflicting feelings. But, the love he felt for her overpowered all the shit Rah was talking.

"Listen, I have some business to handle and I'm going to need you to go and stay with Queen for a few days," he said with all seriousness.

"Why?" She asked, with a puzzled look on her face.

Bentley really didn't know how to explain to her about the vision he had while he was in jail. He didn't want her to look at him funny or think that he was crazy, so he explained it to her to the best of his ability.

"Listen, I think Rah has been behind a lot of shit concerning me, even some of the way I've been acting towards you. I'm not no punk, so I need to go holla at this dude to see if he's man enough to keep it 100," Bentley said.

Before Rika could come up with any words to comfort him, she heard these words ring in her head:

For we wrestle not against flesh and blood, but against principalities, against powers, against the rulers of the darkness of this world, against spiritual wickedness in high places.
(Ephesians 6:12 KJV)

She spoke them to Bentley.

"What does that mean?" He asked her.

"It means, there's a greater force working through him, so you have to fight a different fight and the fight is spiritual not natural," Rika tried to explain.

However, in all reality, she didn't know where all this was coming from. It was almost like something rose up out of her and was speaking right through her. Bentley was clueless. He had no understanding of what she was speaking, all he knew was he was about to strap up and get at this clown -- and if his homies wanted some, they could get it too. Since Bentley had been home, Rika found herself praying like never before.

"Father, in the name of Jesus, I come to you boldly, but as humble as I know how, asking you first to forgive me of all my sins known and unknown. Forgive me for my thoughts and my actions. Forgive me for not leaning and depending on you like I really should. God, please, help my unbelief, but most of all, Lord, create in me a clean heart and renew in me a right spirit. I plead the blood over anything that is not like You in our lives, and ask you now to cancel out any spirit that tries to come up against us, in Jesus' name. Amen."

Bentley would just sit in awe as he watched Rika transform like a butterfly in its cocoon stage. He really enjoyed watching her move around in her true glory. This was fascinating to him because that was something that he had never witnessed before. Rika was beautiful. And, not just her natural beauty either. She was beautiful in all areas that he could think of.

Bentley was ready to do a life sentence with her once he put all that unnecessary foolishness behind him. Rika had a few things that she needed to rid herself of as well, the only difference was she had decided to take a different approach about it. She didn't know much about God and His real characteristics, but she was going to give it a try.

Bomb answered her phone on the third ring. It was 3:45 a.m. *Who could possibly be calling at this hour?*

"Hello," she answered in a rude tone.

"It's time. Your ticket is already at the airport. I need you to leave ASAP." The caller hung up.

Bentley had been laying real low these last few weeks, but tonight he decided to make his move while Rika was sleep. He crept out of bed real easy and went in the living room where he had stored his bag full of all the things that he needed. First, he checked his 40-caliber glock and made sure it was fully loaded. Then, made sure his gloves were in reach as he slid on his all black sweat suit with his black Timbs. He decided to have Fatima to meet him around the corner so he wouldn't be spotted coming up the street. They were coasting down Hydraulic headed south on their way to the McArthur Park apartments.

Bentley instructed Fatima to hit the lights when they pulled in. They found a parking spot and killed the engine. They both exited the car slowly, looking around both ways. Bentley motioned for Fatima to look over the fence in the trailer park next to the apartments where Rah lived, and the lights were on.

What Bentley didn't know was Rika wasn't no dummy. She was awake the whole time, and waited until he was out the door to spring into action. She too was keeping some things from him. She was secretly talking to her brother Rodge and his homeboy Times One about Rah and all the things that had been going down from day one.

A few days earlier, she had Rodge bring her some arsenal of her own because she had a strange feeling something was about to go down, but she didn't want to alarm Bentley. Rika pulled up in the trailer park across the street from the apartments and decided to walk and come out on the other side so she could get a better look. While she was trying to figure out what was going on, she saw Bentley and Fatima walk up to a double-wide mobile home and walk straight in.

What the fuck? She thought to herself. *This nigga been playing me this whole time. He still fucking with this bitch!*

Rika's blood was running hot. She stood there for a minute in disbelief, once the initial shock wore off she pulled her 380 compact pistol out of her waist and was headed towards the double wide.

When Bentley and Fatima stepped on the front porch, the door opened up for them and Rah was waiting to let them in. Once they entered, Bentley realized he had been set up. He suspected Fatima was in on it when he looked over his shoulder and Fatima had her 9mm raised. *She is ready to blow my brains out.* All Bentley could do was laugh.

"For real? This how we doing it now?" He asked, trying to stall for time.

"Yeah. Rah told me all about the shit you been doing. You're the reason I got robbed. You set it all up! You had plans all along to kill me and collect the insurance money because you knew I had you down as the beneficiary over my policy," she said with the gun shaking in her hand.

"What the hell are you talking about? How was I supposed to know you even had a policy? You never told me that," he said, trying to reason with her.

Before she could come to grips with that truth, Rah interrupted, "That's neither here nor there. Did you really think you were coming in here and demanding some answers from me about who the hell I am? Who do you think you are? You always thought you were better than me. But, the truth is, you're really jealous of me," he said, trying to convince himself more than trying to convince Bentley.

By this time, Fatima realized Rah had played on her emotional state of mind. He had caught her when she was vulnerable, when she was feeling real down and out about herself. He didn't say two words to her when her self-esteem was through the roof. But, just like a tiger goes after the calf left by the flock, he approached her because she was perceived too weak to fight alone. She decided to turn the gun on Rah.

"You tricked me! This was all so you could get back at Bentley. The truth is simple. You're the jealous one. You're full of hate and deceit," Fatima screamed.

"Shut up!" Rah's voiced sounded off through the house.

When Fatima realized that this battle was not hers to fight, she knew she was in over her head. Bentley stood there frozen because he thought he was the one who was supposed to be holding the gun and asking all the questions. But, in a flash, he knew he needed to think quickly. Just then, Fatima raised her gun even higher and aimed it at Rah's head.

Boom! Boom! Boom!

As Rika was walking up to the double wide, she heard a round of gunshots. She ducked behind the bushes in the trailer next door.

"Oh, God! Please, protect him. Please, God," she prayed.

Rika could hear the neighbor's dogs barking in the distance. She decided it was time to move in a little closer when she heard more gunshots.

"Forget this. I'm going in. Lord, cover me with your blood."

Rika peeked her head up from out of the bushes, and all she could see was shadows moving throughout the house. She tip-toed onto the porch and, once she got closer to the door, all she saw was Fatima's brains splattered all over the place.

Out of nowhere, a pecan-complexioned chick came from out of the back room making her Lama sound off, hitting Fatima several times in the head before she even hit the ground. Bentley hit the floor and bear crawled out of the line of fire. He hid behind the counter in the kitchen until he heard footsteps coming his way. That's when he started shooting. He could hear Rah talking to a female, but he couldn't recognize her voice.

"Kill him, because if you don't, he's going to expose us to everybody and then there will be no us anymore. I've worked too hard to build my kingdom, and I refuse to have it torn down by some punk that don't even know who he is," Rah said in a rage.

Just then, Bentley looked at the door and couldn't believe his eyes. *Rika? How the hell did she find me?* He was mad but relieved at the same time. Once their eyes connected, Rika was trying to read his expression. She gave him a once over and realized he had been shot in the shoulder.

She mouthed, "You've been shot."

He shook his head. Right at that moment, Rah spotted her. It was starting to feel like a deja vu of the vision Bentley had in jail, but this was real life and shit just wasn't about to go down like that.

"Get her," Rah yelled.

By this time, a supernatural strength came out of nowhere. In a swift motion, Bentley jumped up running and shooting at the same time. Rika had already started making her pistol sing. Bentley shot Rah in the chest, and he flew back into the girl who was lethal with her game. This gave them time to make their getaway.

As Bentley and Rika were running, they could hear Rah demanding, "Go get them," coughing after each word.

Rika lead Bentley in the same direction that she came from.

"Stop, wait a minute," Bentley said out of breath.

His shoulder was bleeding real bad, so Rika decided to put his other arm over her shoulder to help balance him.

"Come on. We can't stop or they're going to kill us," she said with her voice shaking.

She quickly tried to scoop him up and drag him across Hydraulic where she had left her car. As soon as they got it started and pulled out, they saw a car heading straight towards them. She swerved out of the way then realized it was the opposition.

"GO! GO! GO!" Bentley yelled.

Rika looked in her rearview mirror and the other car was busting a u-turn in the middle of the street.

"Game on bitches," Rika said out loud.

She put the pedal to the floor, headed north, and jumped on I-35 heading toward the city. But whoever was driving the car behind them was coming up on them pretty quickly.

Boom! Boom! Boom!

The back window shattered, causing Rika to swerve across the highway.

"You gotta do better than that," she laughed.

By this time, Bentley had regained his strength and was reloading his glock. Just as he was about to lean out of the window and clap back, the car rear-ended them, causing them to spin out of control. The driver of the other car must not have estimated the distance between them well because both cars collided into each other and both went over the median. By the time Bentley's car stopped rolling, Rika was swung through the front windshield. Lying there trying to get her bearings together, she remembered Bentley.

Rika tried to roll onto her side, but the pain was almost unbearable. Coughing from all the smoke and fumes, she tried to locate the car she was in when suddenly she heard moaning coming from behind the smoke.

"Bentley!"

She cried out in a giant voice. When she didn't get an answer, she tried it again, this time getting up on her feet.

"Bentley," she screamed.

Once the dust cleared, she realized she was walking up on the other car. She reached in her waist and pulled out her 22 automatic that she had as a spare (just in case). She eased up to the car and almost fainted when she saw the driver of the car was Bomb. She was so confused. Rah was in the passenger side with his eyes wide open with the death stare and blood trickling down his face. Rika looked back at Bomb and old memories came flashing before her eyes of all the times she belittled and treated her fucked up. All of those emotions rushed in like a flood.

With tears, she began to scream out in a rage, "You conniving bitch! All theses years you had me confused, afraid and ashamed!"

Without a second thought, she gripped her strap and let five slugs rest in Bomb's head. In the backseat were three men, two looked like Rah's twins. But when she tried to get a closer look, it appeared that they both had birth defects that made their faces look deformed. Rika also noticed there was a guy in the back with a long ponytail who had a big gash in his head. Suddenly, she remembered Bentley again. She rushed over to the car where he was. The groaning that she heard was coming from him.

"Help me," he said.

Rika noticed that one of his arms was pinned under the car. She tried to push the car off but she just didn't have enough strength to do it. She got on her knees beside him to see if she could dig his arm free but nothing. Bentley was going in and out of consciousness.

"Stay woke, baby. You can't fall asleep," she said, slapping his face gently yet firmly.

"I can't help it. Please, go try to find some help from somewhere."

"No," she said, "I'm not leaving you," as she begin to cry, "God please help us! Please!"

At that point, Rika became angry. She jumped up and tried to push the car off of his arm again.

This time, he screamed, "GRRRRRRRRR!"

"What?" She asked in a nervous voice.

"You're making the car move. Just keep rocking it back and forth and I will see if I can release my arm."

Just as Bentley said those words, the vision came back to him and he realized he had to get his hand free. And, they were successful. As they walked along the freeway, not one person stopped. Rika decided it was time to rest for a minute because one side of him was dead weight and he was becoming too heavy for her. They sat down by a pole. She rested her head on her knees and began to cry. But, as she was crying, she heard a song that the church folk used to sing way back in the day and she began to sing it out loud.

> *"I need thee. Oh! I need thee. Every hour, I need thee. Oh bless, bless me now, my savior. I come to thee."*

Just then, she decided to look up. She realized the pole they were resting on had a hospital sign attached to it. It was that moment that she realized that He was the same God that worked for Queen when she called on Him, and that He didn't have any respect of person. Once they made it to the hospital, Rika decided to leave Bentley outside so she could go in and get a wheelchair and tell the doctors and nurses that they need help.

When Rika got to the front counter to speak with the nurse, she said, "My husband is out there and he is badly wounded. We need help right away! Please, hurry!"

The nurse just sat there looking at her like she didn't speak English. So Rika repeated herself, this time she yelled it. It seemed like everybody in the hospital stopped and looked at her.

"Forget it!"

Rika decided to take one of the wheelchairs and bring him in herself. Once she got outside, Bentley was shivering and talking all out the side of his head.

"Don't touch me! You trying to kill me! Help," he screamed.

"Come on, baby. We got to get you some help," she tried to convince him, but he tried to swing at her a few times.

She thought to herself, *Even in a hurt person's weakest moments, they still try to muster up enough strength to hurt the person closest to them.* She knew she had to be firm and forceful at this point, so she snatched him up with all her might and pushed him in the wheelchair. As she rolled him in, she could see people's eyes get wide, like they had never seem blood before. The funny-looking nurse still made them have a seat while she talked to the doctor.

As she sat there, Bentley leaned his head on her shoulder. It wasn't until that moment that Rika began to feel pain shooting from every part of her body and it caused her to cry out, "ARGHHHHH!" The pain was so excruciating, she became light-headed. She had been so busy making sure Bentley was alright that she hadn't paid any attention to her own injuries.

As she looked up, she noticed the nurse pointing at her. The doctor looking over at them was shaking his head as if there was nothing he could do for them. Even the people sitting in the waiting room sat there with disgusting looks on their faces. Rika mustered up enough strength to stand to her feet.

"We're getting the hell out of here. These people are not even equipped to treat our injuries," she said trying to keep from passing out.

"Baby, what are we going to do? If we leave, we might die." Bentley stated.

"Well, if we stay here, we're going to die anyway. It don't make sense for us to sit in the lobby and die anyway. Let's go," she said, barely pushing the wheelchair out the door.

As she walked out of the lobby, she noticed the people sitting there had no real injuries. They were being treated for minor cuts and bruises. *No wonder we were being looked at like foreigners.* The people didn't have an eye to see how badly they were hurt so, instead of sending them to a hospital that could help, they sat there pointing and whispering.

As soon as they got outside, the sun was barely coming up. Rika looked back and forth trying to see which direction she should go. She noticed the sun was beaming on this building about a half block down. She squinted to see what it was. As big as day, she saw the word "EMERGENCY."

She tried to push Bentley as fast as she could. Before she could reach the entrance, she locked the wheelchair and said, "Wait right here so I can go get us some help. You're becoming too heavy for me to push. I'll be right back."

She kissed him on the cheek and tried to bitterly drag herself through the automatic doors.

As soon as the nurses saw her, they sprung into action. It was at that moment Rika collapsed on the floor. With all the breath she had left in her, she told the physician, "NO! My husband is out there. He's worse off than me. Please, go help him."

She tried to get off the stretcher, but the physician gently but firmly laid her back down.

"What about your own needs? You can't be of any help to him if you don't get treated yourself right?"

All the while he was calming her down, he hadn't said a word to his staff about Bentley. All he was doing was commanding things with his presence. She noticed the room became very calm and still. At that moment, she looked up into the eyes of her physician. There was so much compassion, love and peace in his eyes. She was still trying to speak when she heard:

> *Casting all your care upon him;*
> *For he careth for you.*
> *(1Peter 5:7 KJV)*

It was at that moment that she surrendered everything. It felt like she had been out of it for months. When she finally opened her eyes, Queen and Nila were right by her side. Nila kissed her all over her face.

"Momma, you okay?" She asked.

Rika nodded her head yes. Queen could tell Rika was worried about Bentley, so she said, "He's fine."

Rika tried to play it off, "What?"

Before Queen could finish speaking, two police officers came in the room.

"Hi," one said.

"Are you Rika Jordan?" The other asked.

"Yes," Rika said, trying to sit up.

"No, just relax. We're here to let you know that we found your car and the suspects that were involved in this hideous crime. We are here to inform you that all four parties that were involved are deceased," the first officer said.

"Don't you mean all five parties?" Rika asked.

"No, ma'am. There were only four people in the vehicle. One female and three males," he responded.

"You don't understand. I saw them with my own eyes. What about the guy with the ponytail?"

The officers looked at each other and back at Rika like she was delusional.

"Ma'am, just know you don't have to worry. The people that tried to harm you and your husband are all deceased. Now try not to worry too much and get some rest," the second officer said.

With that, they opened the door and walked out. But before the door closed, Rika thought her eyes were deceiving her but they weren't. Two nurses were wheeling a guy into the operating room. Rika couldn't see his face. But, as soon as they turned the corner, she saw his ponytail and the door closed.

Epilogue

Hello, readers. I would like to shed some light on this book, as well as help you understand what it means (or, should I say, what it looks like) to "escape my own prison." A lot of people have created some form of prison for themselves, and don't fully understand what it means to be free. In other words, there are more people in prison that are free than there are walking around on the streets. Being locked up is not just a physical thing. It's also mental and emotional.

Some have been locked up due to unforeseen circumstances, and others by simply not making good choices -- or what I like to call "Blindfolded Decisions." Whatever category you may be in, there's always a way out so don't allow yourself to believe any different.

You see, all my life I made those blindfolded decisions. And, due to this decision-making, I became a 13-year-old mom and a homeless drug addicted teen. When you really pay close attention to the people I chose to associate with, one could recognize my insecurities and weakness. Those experiences can now let me put a face on some of the links to the chains that held me captive for a huge part of my life.

With that being said, let's take Bomb for instance. Bomb was a representation of the confusion that was often present in my thoughts, which allowed fear (Bomb) to set in and cripple me for many years. As sad as it is to say, when fear takes root, it opens the doors for all sorts of things to grow in your life. All it needs is a seed to grow from, and we all know "anything you feed will grow." So, I fed confusion and fear for so long that I made myself believe that I wasn't good enough or worthy of anything good.

That caused me to have a very distorted view on life, and that's when I was introduced to "Wanda." Wanda happened to expose the lust that was just waiting to be watered so it could grow. When lust set in, this demon was one that grew faster than any addiction I ever had. It caused me to go down real fast.

In my mind, you see, lust is something that's not always seen. We walk around with lustful thoughts in our minds, homes, churches and schools. But, it's deadly and very lethal to the process of spiritual growth. Only God can purge and free you from this type of weight. I know for me, He had to teach me what it really meant to "renew my mind" (*Romans 12:2*).

That's why, if you notice, Bomb had a problem with Wanda and tried to kill her in the story. But, the truth of the matter is, these three spirits were at war in my thoughts all the time:

Lust, Fear and Confusion. By the time I connected with my husband, he was trying to escape from his own solitary confinement. That is why Rahim happens to present himself as a friend but, in the background of things, he represents hurt.

My husband happened to suffer a great deal of hurt (Rah) from a very early age. I often refer to it as being "crippled at birth" because it was nothing that he did, it was just unforeseen circumstances he endured. Hurt makes you look out of angry, selfish and bitter eyes. And, it's hard to love and be loved by anyone when you let deep wounds go untreated for too long. Hurt (Rah) is never a friend. It has a way of isolating you and making you feel like no one understands you, and sometimes it can even lead to self-destruction.

Now, let me explain the different hospitals. The first one represents a church. This type of church is only equipped to handle simple things like what's on the outside, but it's not equipped to deal with real wounds. They want to help, but they don't have any spiritual sight to look past the smiles, pretty hats, nice suites, and fat wallets and really focus on the real needs of God's people. There are so many people broken and hurt in the church that just sit there week after week wondering when their change is going to come.

That was the case for me and my husband. We attended church week after week, and were about to die at the watch of a physician's assistant (a pastor). That's why it took God to tug at my spirit for me to move, get up, and go where my soul mattered. So, not only could I get the help (The Word) that I needed but, I would be able to be treated, healed, delivered and set free by the only one who could do it -- God Himself.

But, what I had to learn upon arrival was that I couldn't carry my husband any further because I needed to be healed myself. As long as you let your wounds go untreated, it's humanly impossible to try to help someone else. I don't care who it is.

Let me shed some light on Ponytail for you too. He's the thorn in our side. He's that sin that just won't go anywhere. We have begged and pleaded for God to remove this one thing! And, just like God:

> And he said unto me, **My grace is sufficient for thee: for my strength is made perfect in weakness.** Most gladly therefore will I rather glory in my infirmities, that the power of Christ may rest upon me.
> *(2 Corinthians 12:9 KJV)*

So, despite whatever prison you've created for your life, just know it's not permanent but temporary. Join me in the next chapter in my life! **<u>From The Ghetto To The Throne: Joy Comes In The Morning</u>**.

The Art & Artist

An 8-year commitment where more than 50% was created in a matter of eight weeks, **FROM THE GHETTO TO THE THRONE: Escaping My Own Prison** is Secret Bryant's first release from a dual series of non-fiction that seeks to remind readers  that no bad times last forever and show how God's grace can repeatedly be seen even in the worst of times. The life-inspired debut was penned with the hope of testifying to younger and older adults about the unlimited willingness of God to forgive, protect, heal and inform sinners just as He does saints.

FROM THE GHETTO TO THE THRONE: Escaping My Own Prison by Secret Bryant is available for order worldwide via Kindle as an e-book for $9.95, or as a softback for $19.95 (plus shipping and taxes) from bricks-and-mortar and online book retailers including Barnes & Noble, your local bookstore, and Amazon.Com.

AUTHOR

The owner / operator of Southern Style & Barber LLC in Portland, Oregon, **Secret Bryant** is a native of Los Angeles, California, and proud Washington State resident. A Christian wife and mother of five who spoils her 10 grandchildren, Secret is a graduate of WATC and she completed journalism studies at Wichita State University in Kansas.

She became a licensed cosmetologist in 2008 after graduating Phagan's School of Hair Design in Portland. In 2010, Southern Styles & Barber was featured in *West Coast Magazine* in celebration of Secret's new business and multicultural clientele.

"I'm proud of my salon, my ministry, and my ability to really overcome," the equestrian admits. "I'm most proud of my 20-year marriage and my children."

The author's hobbies also include traveling, socializing, shopping and fellowshipping with other Christians. Secret also enjoys volunteering with Sistah 2 Sister, an organization mentoring girls ages 13-21 to empower them with skills including self-esteem and personal hygiene.

The entrepreneur and her husband are presently planning to enroll at Portland State University this autumn. Together, they will study marriage and family therapy. Their long-term goals are to obtain doctoral degrees and open their own marriage and family counseling practice in Vancouver, Washington.

A former resident of Texarkana, Texas, the author of **FROM THE GHETTO TO THE THRONE:**  **Escaping My Own Prison** is currently working to close the dual series by completing her next work soon. **From The Ghetto To The Throne: Joy Comes In The Morning** is projected to be available for worldwide purchase by the end of 2016.

www.sostylesandbarber.com

Tee,

Keep being you and don't EVER change the world needs to experience the authentic you!!! I hope our story inspires you to reach for the stars the sky has NO!!! Limits 😊

2 Corinthians 5:17

BWyatt

Made in the USA
Middletown, DE
22 March 2021